# HOME
## IS MY GARDEN

Dorothy Hammond Innes is the wife of Hammond Innes the author and shares his travels, including his sailing – she is a member in her own right of the Royal Ocean Racing Club. Her grandfather emigrated from the Scottish border (she is a kinswoman of Sir Walter Scott and Andrew Lang) to Australia, where her father was born. Her mother ran away from her English home to be a missionary in India; her parents met there, but were in Shanghai when she was born.

Dorothy Hammond Innes was an actress before her marriage and her first writing was for the theatre; she had plays produced for a Sunday Night at the Saville Theatre in London, at the Edinburgh Festival and at the Belgrade Theatre, Coventry. Her first book, *Occasions*, recorded travels with her husband in search of material for his novels. Her second book, *What Lands Are These?* (available in Fontana), describes three major journeys made since – to Africa, Papua New Guinea, Pakistan – and the story of their forestry lodge in Wales.

Brenda Moore studied art for ten years before marrying the distinguished painter Leonard Campbell-Taylor R.A. After twenty-six non-painting years she began again working in portraiture – one of her husband is in the National Portrait Gallery – and she has since sold paintings in many countries. In 1982 her exhibition of flower paintings was the first one-man show at the Barbican.

# HOME
# IS MY GARDEN

## Dorothy Hammond Innes

### Drawings by Brenda Moore

Fontana/Collins

First published in Great Britain by Harvill Press 1984
First issued in Fontana Paperbacks 1986

Copyright © in the text Dorothy Hammond Innes 1984
Copyright © in the drawings Brenda Moore 1984

Made and printed in Great Britain by
William Collins Sons & Co. Ltd, Glasgow

Acknowledgement is made to the following for
permission to quote from copyright material:
Macmillan Publishers Ltd for 'The Darkling
Thrush' and 'The Oxen' by Thomas Hardy; The
Society of Authors as the literary representative
of the estate of John Masefield for an extract from
an untitled poem by John Masefield; J. M. Dent
Ltd for an extract from 'Fern Hill' by Dylan
Thomas.

TO
REG * VERENA * NORA

# CONTENTS

'Oh Year, grow slowly.'  KATHERINE TYNAN

'Rien ne se perd, rien ne se crée, on
redécouvre.'

MADAME SONIA BLETCH
of Mijanou Restaurant

The assumption of this book is that the reader is a
friend who comes round the garden with me,
becoming familiar with its changing face as the
seasons pass over it; becoming – I hope – fond of it.
Then we come back to the house with a trug of
vegetables, sit down in the kitchen and decide what
to do with them.

I hope it comes over as a happy book; it should,
because it is written with love and pleasure, as a
celebration.

DOROTHY HAMMOND INNES

# ...BUT A HOME!

'Have you a home, or do you travel all the time?' This question always stuns me, and I hear it quite often on our journeys; so does the second question, 'But are you ever there?' This book is the answer to both those questions. I have tried to record the journeys by which I am most haunted in my first two books. This is the other half of our lives, the home from which we set out, and to which we return. And the home-coming is always as exciting as the setting-out – which is as it should be, I think!

Perhaps I should explain why I cannot take a home for granted.

I never had a home as a child, and my mother, I think, grew up feeling herself the odd-one-out as her mother died when she was three, and her father soon married again. When her step-brother and step-sister began to grow up she was rather pushed out. So she ran away to India to become a missionary – leaving the customary note on the mantelpiece. She became familiar with travel, but to have a home . . . that was the dream.

My own father died when I was six months old, I don't remember him. My mother sketched in his roving life for me in relevant, revealing flashes; and told me, too, how my grandfather had left the Scottish Border for Australia, where he has left something of a legend; then went to Italy and became a friend of Garibaldi, and wrote an article for *The Times* of London which first jolted the British Government and British people into realizing Garibaldi mattered. So I took it for granted that people moved about the world. But to have a home!

Shortly after my father's death the money he had left, just enough for us to live on, disappeared in some crash. So my mother, quite untrained, had to earn our living (no Government hand-outs then). I realize now that she took any little jobs she could get, anywhere, that enabled her to keep me with her, as I was all that was left of her life. We were always moving, and I always cried the last night, thinking 'I shall never see this again, or this, or this.' I remember my mother, packing, saying mystified, 'But I thought you didn't even like this place?' The only constant things in these years were our luggage, and a silver-framed photograph of my father on a lovely horse.

Our luggage was sprinkled through with treasures – incongruous in the sequence of drab lodgings we occupied, or as migrants in other people's houses; each treasure was wrapped in its own protective covering of lace or embroidery or silky-fine cashmere: tiny silver pepper pots; the white ostrich feathers she had worn when she was presented; two little gilt-framed photographs, one of her in a white dress standing on a big lawn in front of a long white house, the other of her and my father sitting in a drawing room. These had *CHOWRINGEE* written in faint ink on the back. These dainty ghosts from another life she clung to, I have them still. And she gave me treasures of a different kind: that we were related to Sir Walter Scott, a famous Borderer who had written splendid adventure stories which I would read when I was older; and to Andrew Lang.

On trains, if she got out to see about the luggage, or to make some enquiry, I was in agony for fear the train started before she came back. What would become of me? This fear of being left, of being lost, I have never outgrown.

Yet somehow she created magic for me. My birthday tea was always splendid, though never twice in the same place – a lace cloth, tiny candles in miniature square brass candlesticks, and a wonderfully iced cake. I remember my first primroses, and picking wild daffodils in a wood; walking in the snow, and building a snowman. On walks she would read to me. I can still see her, slowing her steps to mine, her head bent to the book, reading *Alice through the Looking Glass* in, I think, the outskirts of Liverpool. For me the White Knight always rides against those cold grey streets. Probably we walked so much because we hadn't anywhere warm to sit at that time. When I was tired and asked to turn home, I can hear her saying bitterly, 'Go "back" you mean? Not "home". It isn't home, it's only back.'

I had a glamorous aunt, my father's sister, who was very fond of my mother, with whom we used to stay sometimes. (Unfortunately she died when I was about seven.) Her personal maid used to make me exquisite clothes, which I thought boring and wished they'd give me toys. But this aunt had a beautiful house in a very beautiful garden, in which I played. This was the first big garden of my life, and it was an enchanted world in which no harm could come, set apart from the harsh scramble of life. I became a different person. I remember the white seat almost hidden under purple clematis, the pools, the heliotrope beds, the smell of lemon-verbena, the lawn with its great spreading cedar tree under which I held dolls' tea parties.

Quite recently, driving in Kent, I realized we were near the place, and I wanted to show Ralph at least the outside. I couldn't find it where I knew it must be, then I realized the road had been pushed back, and the house was now the area's Municipal Offices. The garden, which had lain behind the house, was blotted out, completely built over with a housing estate.

Towards the end of my schooldays, my mother out of her own earnings achieved a flat of great charm near the Downs in Eastbourne, and bought some beautiful things for it, which I still have. I loved this flat – my first home – as if it were a person. But I left it to run away to London on a wet Monday morning to go on the stage, and that was the end of our shared life. Many lifetimes later, it seems, she came here to spend her last ten years with us.

Now I have a home of my own I can never take it for granted, but hold it insecurely, with a sense of wonder, 'Can this really be mine?'

# FINDINGS

As the main part of this book may seem suspiciously serene, perhaps I should explain it was not always so.

When Ralph came back from the war we had an old and beautiful cottage in Wiltshire which was just two rooms up and two down, with a separate kitchen. Ralph turned down the offer of his old job – in journalism – back, and set up as a writer. The cupboards filled with typing paper and the clothes piled on chairs, and he wrote *The Lonely Skier* and *Maddon's Rock* sitting in an armchair with the typewriter on his knee. *The Lonely Skier* sold its film rights and *Maddon's Rock* did well as a BBC serial, and both were successful as books, so our only reading became house agents' lists, and we combed Southern England for a possible house. We learned to interpret the cosy idiom of house agents, but there seemed to be nothing between decaying manor houses, demanding a fortune in repairs, heating and staff, and cottages, too small and noisy to work in.

We were beginning to despair; I remember saying, 'Let's spend the money on a wonderful journey, there isn't a house for us.' We went to Norway, stayed on the off-shore islands, crossed the Sanct Paul glacier, went round Nord Cap in a little steamer – material used in *The Blue Ice* and later in *The White South*.

We had seen this Suffolk house, looking through beautiful gates at the end of the drive. It was not (of course!) on the market, but we remembered it. We had been househunting in company with Ralph's agent, Spencer Curtis Brown, and his wife, who were looking for a much larger house for his company – which they found. Then a letter was forwarded to us in Norway from Jean Curtis Brown – she was still being circularized by house agents – enclosing a brochure and saying: 'Isn't this the beautiful house we saw through the gates in that little medieval village?' It had come on the market, so the search was over.

We moved in December. We only had furniture to sprinkle through a few rooms, no curtains or carpets. The house had no main services. The plants supplying water and electricity had been good in their time, but were now old. The electric plant supplied lighting, but not power, so couldn't be used for cleaning or heating equipment. It needed starting up every night, but stopped itself when the last light was switched off. You had to leave it a moment, then switch on to make sure the plant really was off. Sometimes guests didn't realize this – Peter Wilson, the sports writer, switched on and off too quickly, thus re-starting the engine each time. He kept this up at intervals for an hour, getting frantically worried while the plant became hysterical, so did anyone else kept awake, as the engine was quite noisy. (I, inured to noise by my Shanghai birth, slept through such trivia.)

Quite often during the evening the lights would flutter and die, so we trooped down the drive to the little pump-house beside the garage, and I held a torch while Ralph worked on the plant. Many, many man-hours, and woman-hours, were spent on this. There was a splendid old bell-board in the kitchen, with the names of each room, including the bathrooms, and an alarm beside each to tell which room had summoned attention. It didn't work; I think the wiring in the loft had got tangled, because an irregular jangling of faint bells sometimes happened for no apparent reason.

Baths were not easy; there was a huge black stove in the kitchen which, if fed a sufficient amount of coke, produced enough boiling water to wash an army – it was all or nothing. We finally sold this to a poet who lived in the stables of Borley Rectory, 'The Most Haunted House in England'. He wanted it for growing mushrooms. When he came to fetch it, he took one look and said, 'Your hands are stronger than mine.' So Ralph and a friend of ours moved it for him.

The water pump never failed, giving us lovely soft water from a deep well under our lawn, but of course there was not enough pressure for showers. But the Aga – oh, my darling Aga! This heroic creature made life possible. It was old; young engineers patted it and said, 'They don't make them that quality now!' I'd had grand ideas of replacing it with a new one, but as I was neither a doctor, nor a farmer, I couldn't even get my name on a waiting list. But it had been reconditioned and worked superbly for many years (on solid fuel). Only when we put in central heating did we replace it with a modern oil-burning one, which is cleaner and less trouble, but not such a fine cooking stove.

We were in New York on our first visit to the U.S.A. (celebrating *The White South*, which had sold its film rights to Hollywood, serial rights to that then-great American institution *Saturday Evening Post*, also a Book Club), when a letter arrived for Ralph, in a batch forwarded from home, from the Eastern Electricity Board. It said, 'As your representations have been instrumental in our deciding to bring forward the electrification of the village, we would like to do your house first.' We had to write and say, please leave us till last! I coped with the installation when I came home. Ralph had gone to Canada, making the adventurous journey through the West and the Rockies which produced *Campbell's Kingdom*.

We had a part-time gardener whom we called Snow White (we thought he resembled the nicest of the dwarfs). He had been under-gardener here in the past, but now he was older he had trouble with his tubes, so we did the heavy work. You could see the lovely design of the garden, but it had been neglected for years and it was tantalizing – heart-breaking! – to think what it might be. It seemed on top of us all the time. Then . . .

Verena and her brother Reg came into our lives. Now, they have for so long looked after the house and garden – whether we are here, or whether we are in Papua New Guinea or Alaska – that it is difficult to remember exactly how we found each other.

Verena's sister Marjorie was the first one I knew – a lively, vigorous girl, who really preferred working in the fields (her favourite job in the house was polishing, and she brought her own left-handed potato peeler). She had a natural grace of manner; I remember her putting her head round the door with a message, and thinking: People pay a lot at finishing schools learning how to do that so charmingly. One day she said, 'I've a brother who works at the old aerodrome, but I'm sure he'd come along on Saturday to shift that load of manure for you' (it was waiting out in the lane).

So Reg first walked into the garden that was to become his private kingdom. He gardened for us part-time at first, then his work clearing the site of the aerodrome came to an end, and Ralph asked him if he would like to come to us full-time. 'Funny thing,' he said, 'I'd been wondering to myself whether Mr Hammond Innes might be wanting a full-time man!' So the thought came from both sides.

As a child he had suffered a mastoid in one ear and a double mastoid in the other. It was a medical wonder he could hear at all. It was a greater marvel that growing up in such pain, and in the loneliness of deafness, he developed such an alert, interested, friend-making personality.

As a gardener, he only knew what most country boys know; how to dig well (an excellent basis!) and how to grow a few crops. The round-the-year maintenance of a varied garden rather ambitiously laid out, with all the method, observation and anticipation that it needs, had to be learned. That first Saturday morning when the job was agreed, I remember Ralph borrowed from me and put into his hands Shewell Cooper's *The Complete Gardener* (a fat red book Collins had given me when they published it), saying, 'Of course experience is the only real way to learn, but take this. Don't try to read it through, but as you come to each new process in the garden, look up what he says about it. Then at least you'll have some idea how to set about it, and can see how it works out in practice. My wife and I will help you – we'll make a gardener of you!' Reg took the book home, kept it a long time, and brought it back well-read. Ralph thought it worth taking the afternoons off from writing to work with him in the garden, that first autumn, showing him a variety of basic processes, going over a thing till it became automatic, and he'd soon forget he hadn't always known it! The November evenings drew in, I was typing a play I'd written called *The Leopard*, later produced with Albert Lieven. We were still using the electric plant, which I couldn't start as the engine was too heavy to turn, and Ralph working out of doors till it got dark, didn't turn it on, so I used to finish typing by candle-light.

Reg compared notes with other gardeners, read a gardening magazine; gradually the problems were mastered, the failed crops became successful, the range of things grown increased steadily.

This book shows the result. In addition, he is responsible for the premises during our long absences.

The companionship of our successive Alsatians has been an important part of his life here. They show extraordinary observation in following and anticipating everything he does (glancing out of the window I see he's unloading logs for the house, and close beside him, Yiwara's beautiful head goes up and down, up and down, mentally shifting every log). *Yiwara* is an Aborigine word meaning *track*, either in a literal sense – the way from one waterhole to the next; or a connection between two people – a link. This puppy followed our Australian period, the long pilgrimage ending in the West, from which Ralph wrote *Golden Soak*; and the kennels from which she came had reached 'Y' in their alphabetic registration of litters. She is our first long-haired one, very glamorous. We became involved with Alsatians because my mother, at the beginning of the war, had taken pity on one that was going to be destroyed because his master was ordered overseas. Ever since, one of them has been a member of our household.

One day Marjorie said . . . (so it all comes back to Marjorie? I'd forgotten that), 'I wonder if you ever have any rather special laundry – things that need care? I've a sister who's very good at that sort of thing, very dainty. Her husband is very ill, and she has a little boy so she's tied to the house, but she'd like a little job she could do at home.'

So Verena came to see me. I remember vividly how she sat opposite me at the dining table, and how strong the impact of her calm, her poise, her fresh neatness was, this pretty young woman who had just come from, and was going back to, a home which was at that moment so tragic; beautiful eyes, a lovely skin, a bright lipstick worn like a flag; but it was her control, her spirit in that situation that stayed in my mind.

The laundry was exquisitely done. When her husband died (of leukemia) she came to help me look after the house, Marjorie having moved with her husband to another village. I need say no more about Verena, as she permeates the rest of this book! Except that she re-married, happily.

Nora, the third member of our triumvirate, is a Scot from the

Highlands. She was a trained and experienced secretary, and arrived on our doorstep one morning because, hearing there was a writer in the village, she thought there might be some typing. . . . Years later, as the world-wide ramifications of Ralph's work and our other interests grew up round her, and she handled it all, she sometimes said, 'Little I knew! I came along so innocently, just thinking there'd be manuscripts to type, and a bit of correspondence!' She and her husband had bought a lovely house in the village, and brought up their two children here.

These three, working together, maintained this place both as home and working base, through the years. When we sailed into Istanbul; when we came down to Lima from Machu Pichu; when we flew into Auckland almost hysterical with tiredness; there would be letters from Nora (who wrote such entertaining letters) and sometimes from Verena too, telling us that all was well. Essential 'work' news of course, but also what was out in the garden, what had happened in the village; first how the dog was, whose 'sheep-dog instinct feels we should all work in the same place. As it is she has to go the rounds, looking after Reg in the garden, Verena in the house, me in the study!'

Generally, wherever I am is the only place; I belong to it, forgetting everything else. But sometimes, if I am tired or frightened, or (very occasionally) bored, then I seek reassurance by deliberately sending my mind back to the remembered face of home, and sink into it with infinite luxury.

# THE MONTHS

# JANUARY

# JANUARY

'Cold in the ground, and the deep snow
piled above thee.'

EMILY BRONTË

On 2 January (New Year's Day being a holiday), Reg brought the big trug into the kitchen full of vegetables and salads.

Chicory, salsify, celeriac, sprouts, lettuces, lamb's lettuce, leeks, celery. Red and green cabbages hang in the woodshed. Potatoes, onions, shallots and carrots are in the store cupboard; boxes of mustard-and-cress in the greenhouse – fifteen things altogether. There is parsley and fennel under cloches. On the larder shelf are the bottles of plums and tomatoes and gooseberries Verena preserved last summer, and all her lovely jams. Gourds kept for winter soups. Still a tin full of hazelnuts, keeping full and moist in their husks – say twenty crops not counting herbs. And of course the later apples. . . .

It's very unusual for us to bring in so many crops at the same time, and count them as if preparing for a siege. But the weather forecast was violent, so in a lull between two periods of freeze-up, Reg thought it wise to bring in as much as he could. Usually he just brings what I want to cook that evening, and some salads for lunch.

January is the giant of the months. Partly because it seems to begin after Christmas and go on for ever; but also because it can strike blows that disorganize one's life, and transform the familiar, welcoming garden into a strange black-and-white Brueghel world.

While the snow was at its deepest, smoothing out the garden, the moon was at the full. It rose like a huge piece of money at the end of the drive. I had never before seen a hard, frightening moon. At the other end of the night and the opposite end of the house, it glared in to our bedroom window at seven o'clock in the morning, still lighting the whole white countryside, a polished silver disc, glittering out of an indigo sky.

When we first came here, a neighbour who had known the place a long time said, 'I like this garden best in winter, it has architectural beauty.' I hardly knew what she meant at the time, but I learnt, gradually. She was looking out from the landing window, from which you see the pattern most clearly.

The house had been a barn for a period, and the ground round it just a rough field. Not until someone showed us a picture of it, in a book called *Old Suffolk Houses*, did we realize it had had a previous existence. The garden as we know it had been laid out by a previous owner in consultation with an architect from the Royal Horticultural Society, of which she was a member. It is roughly a figure-of-eight, narrowest opposite the house where the stream, which is one of our boundaries, curves towards us; then ballooning out at either end. We are on the edge of the village, and beyond us are fields. The house (wisely placed) stands well above the stream, and the garden terraces down to it on four levels. From end to end it is divided into little gardens of different character, after the charming eighteenth-century fashion of thinking a garden, like a house, should have rooms. There is a rose garden opposite the house, lying on the middle level between the terrace and the river bank where daffodils are naturalized under the trees; a 'Dutch' garden of four large square beds round a Charles I sundial; three little lily ponds running down to the stream; and immediately below the house a long line of rockeries broken by steps and paved paths. Two lines of tall climbing roses cross the garden. At either end is a lawn, and beyond each lawn are big trees – protection and background – framing it.

The snow deepened, layer upon layer. We hadn't had a winter as severe as this since the year Joy Adamson stayed with us – 20 January, I remember, because it was her birthday, and the anniversary of the day Elsa died. It was also the anniversary of my mother's death. We were cut off, shut in by the weather. Ralph piled logs on the fire and opened a bottle of champagne, and we drank to my mother, to Elsa, and to Joy on her birthday. Years later, she told me she still had the cork of that bottle. During the evening we thought we heard a knock at the door; we had an Alsatian puppy too young to identify sounds or feel responsible for them. I went to the door, not imagining anyone could have come on such a night. There was no one, but a flash of colour caught my eye; in the most sheltered corner was a lovely little arrangement – a small log, with two red candles stuck to it in plasticine, moss, holly, a ribbon, little flowers tucked into the moss, snowdrops, a couple of primroses, a sprig of wallflower, hyacinths from a pot plant. There was a note in writing I knew, from a wonderful Romany woman who lived in the village; she and my mother had made friends. The note just said 'today we must be remembering'.

The next morning Ralph photographed Joy crouching in the snow, her notorious leopardskin coat startling against the whiteness, playing with the puppy.

When at last the snow thinned and shrank to a few patches in deep shade, I went round the garden. Yiwara, our long-haired Alsatian bitch, niece of the one Joy had known, pushed past me, lifting her head and drinking the air to learn what scents the frost had not killed. Who had been in her territory – rabbits, a hare, a fox, ducks from the stream in the early morning, a squirrel, a pheasant? The hedgehogs were hibernating, and the moles far underground; had a poaching cat come to dig up her bones?

I set out gingerly, like an animal creeping out after hibernation. It had been too cold, too slippery, too buried. Now it was emerging, green again, and could be recognized. The first aconites have pushed their knuckles above the ground. A mass of daffodil spikes are two inches up at the back of the border and round the pools. Two absurd clumps of pansies have never stopped blooming since last spring. The prunus autumnalis seems to have lost its next lot of buds, but the branches I cut before the cold spell started are still frothy-white on top of a dresser in the kitchen.

There is so much colour in the winter garden. All the mahonia bushes are shining bronze, a line of santolina is silver; many shades of green – the holly very dark, the lawsonia a fluffy blue column, the low box hedges round the sundial beds almost golden-green like the new growth on the yews, Now the tall trees are bare, you can see through the tracery of their branches the gabled half-timbered houses of the village, some white, some red, blazing to crimson at sunset.

I cannot go to the kitchen garden across the bridge because it is under water; when the snow melts the stream always floods on the further side, which lies lower. Now the kitchen garden is a lake, with two beautiful ducks swimming between the brussels sprouts.

I'm cold. It's nice to go into the warm kitchen. What is left of the things Reg brought in at New Year? Our regular working-day lunch consists of soup, home-made bread, which Verena bakes from local stone-ground flour, a varied cheese board and a salad.

Gourds saved from summer, golden like pumpkins – or frilly-white custard marrows – are a wonderful basis for soup. Only a strong man can cut through the rind, but the inside, firm and juicy, we slice with onion, potato, carrot, parsnip – whatever there is – simmer till tender, then put through the liquidizer, bring to the consistency of cream with stock or milk, add nutmeg or mace as well as pepper and salt; if no stock, I add a spoonful of marmite, and always top of milk or a little cream. These gourds produce a soup the colour of lobster bisque, with a distinctive and delicious flavour.

French onion soup I make whenever I have a good stock. Mine is a rather peasant version, the onions not cut too small – the large, sweet, tender onions are best. I simmer them in butter till tender, sprinkle a very little flour, just to absorb the butter; then add the stock, salt and a lot of pepper, and leave to simmer. Then when the bowls are filled, I put a slice of stale white bread on top of each, cover this thickly with grated cheese, and put in the hot oven till they are brown and crusty. This is how I ate it first, sitting at a table on the pavement outside a little French restaurant in Rabat.

Then there is leek soup; we chop those leeks which are too big for salad, simmer in stock, or water, liquidize with their cooking liquor and make up with milk to the consistency of pale green velvet, add marmite and spices. (A little potato makes it even smoother.)

Really one needn't have the same soup twice in a week, the winter vegetables have such very distinctive flavours. Best of all, I think, is celeriac. Peel and chop and simmer and liquidize, add milk and a little cream, nutmeg and seasoning – put one onion in to cook with it, unless there's a stray chive or spring onion up, or the green young tops of old onions sprouting on the shelf, to sprinkle on top of the bowls before serving. This time it's cream velvet! but it's the celeriac you want to taste, with no distraction except the garnish on top and some cream.

Home-made tomato soup I regard as a luxury – can one ever have a big enough crop of tomatoes to spare one of Verena's bottles for soup, when one needs them to make sauce for spaghetti? Yes, occasionally one can. Then I just drop them in boiling water to skin them, heat some olive oil and soften a chopped onion, squash the tomatoes till the juices run and they are a rough purée. Add brown sugar and basil (alas, dried in winter), and a light stock. Sometimes I put this through the liquidizer, sometimes not. Of course you can add potato or anything else to make more, or thicker, soup, but the less you do to it the better. Even a little is worth it – the sweet tangy taste of summer!

Artichoke soup I make like celeriac. For a parsnip soup I add potato and onion. Seven soups from the winter garden – the weather when one needs soup most.

Verena often takes over the soup-making. I rush to the kitchen and find it smelling delicious, and think about salads. The trouble with winter salads is that they take much longer to prepare than the ever-ready summer salads, and I am always later than I hope, because of an absurd feeling that if I do a job before lunch – 'in the morning' – I have somehow conquered the day better than if I serve lunch in good time, and do the other job after lunch – 'in the afternoon'.

Take coleslaw, for instance; you must grate the firm white cabbage in advance to leave it in salted icy water for a reasonable time, then allow it to drain. I mix in a grated raw onion and a crisp apple (Cox's if possible), and a little French dressing before adding mayonnaise, it combines so much more smoothly. Then I add whatever I have, chopped celery, grated carrot (and in summer cucumber, peppers, tomato, herbs). To make a more substantial dish I mix in a tin of drained tunny, which goes particularly well, and perhaps a few capers. In Brussels, where I discovered coleslaw, they added small strips of lean ham.

Celeriac (the French *céleri-rave*) must also be started in advance.

Verena will have done the arduous part – peeling these rough-looking brown objects, and putting them in lemony water to keep them white. I grate them on a mandoline till I am afraid I shall catch my fingers if I go any further (the remaining pieces are for soup). The grated celeriac must go instantly into boiling water, also with lemon, for a couple of minutes only, off the fire, then under cold water in a colander and left to dry. No good rushing in at the last minute to prepare *céleri-rave*! Unlike potato salad, it doesn't want to be dressed warm, it loses firmness. When cold and as dry as possible, I dress it with mayonnaise into which I've mixed grainy French mustard. I admit that for this, as for cole-slaw and potato salad, I use a bought mayonnaise. Of course it isn't the same, as mayonnaise depends on the flavour of a good olive oil, but life is not long enough to make it every time. A couple of anchovy fillets and a few black olives are a nice garnish to *céleri-rave*, and a green froth of mustard-and-cress round it.

But I discovered a beautifully quick winter salad; leeks – young and delicate, the size of a 2p piece. I find that if you cut them as thin as possible (surprisingly easy with a sharp knife and a good board), they are delicious raw. Even the briefest immersion in hot water relates them to seaweed, and had always put me off so-called leek salads. I pile the wafer-thin white and green slices in a glazed black pottery dish we brought back from the Beau-manière at Les Baux. I find it is best to dress the leeks with olive oil first, then rock salt and black pepper, then a squeeze of lemon juice. If you use a vinaigrette you've mixed already, the leeks occasionally have a burning quality, which never happens with the oil first. Garnish it with mustard-and-cress, grated carrot, chopped nuts, parsley – whatever is handy. We always put a cloche over some of the parsley patch.

I used to despise carrots, but we grow nice ones, and they are so versatile. Finely grated and mixed with a lot – really a lot, not just a garnish – of freshly ground parsley, dressed with a sweet French dressing, they are a delicious extra salad. Long ago, Reg planted carrot seed too late to 'turn in', so he forgot about them, and was surprised to find them, in January, about two inches long, tender and perfect in flavour and texture. Scrubbed, eaten whole and raw and dipped in sour cream, they are delicious, with a nutty crispness like young brazils. Now he repeats this lucky mistake.

Chicory, one of our best winter crops, I try to save for February and March, but you can't leave it too long or it grows through its clamp. When we first came here, a neighbour told us he had worked in Belgium before the war, and learned the triangular cut at the top of the plant when lifted (chicory . . . Belgian *endive* . . . why this international confusion?) which results in tight neat bundles instead of loose leaves. He taught other people, so that during the war this village sent chicory up to Covent Garden, which was cut off from its imported supply. He passed this skill on to Reg; ours is not all as large as the commercially grown, but it is much more delicate in texture and flavour. I chop it into chunks and mix it with grated apple, or segments of orange or grapefruit; or it ekes out the last of a crop of lettuces.

The flood water has disappeared as quickly as it came, leaving the river high, brown, and fast-flowing. Imperceptibly the days lengthen. Frost grips the garden at night, and some mornings the lawns look like silver fur. The mahonias' colour deepens from bronze to crimson, brilliant patches of red all over the garden. In the afternoon it is almost warm on windless days. There is magical contrast in the delicate fresh green of the plants under cloches, and the bare surrounding garden, but the next lettuces, even the lambs' lettuce, are slow to make and are much too small to pick yet.

Reg has begun to bring the cinerarias up to the house from our small greenhouse. Their exotic purples and reds and blues light the hall in the dark days. I mass them on an old Edwardian sauce-pan stand painted white and placed in a corner. He has already planted onion seed (North Holland) in the seed propagator to achieve the huge sweet onions for baking – the same seed sown later out of doors only reaches half the size. He has sown geranium seed, so they will flower this summer, and planted our begonia tubers in boxes of soil.

The evening kitchen is a welcoming place; Yiwara always comes with me and lies in front of the Aga (I have a cousin in Scotland who cooks with two labradors round her ankles). Ralph is still down in the study working; it is a very peaceful time.

The chicory is big enough for hot dishes now. I will make the dish I learned in Brussels, where it was a regular first course for lunch or dinner – chicory with hard-boiled eggs in a white sauce. I add an anchovy fillet to each egg half. The essential in cooking chicory is to do it slowly. The neat bundles are laid head-to-tail in a buttered fireproof dish, sprinkled with lemon juice, salt and pepper, also a little stock or water, as the resultant liquid will make the sauce. Then push the lidded dish to the back of the slow oven, this is best done at teatime. Inspect after a couple of hours, and take out when a fork goes through the thick part – it should be firm, not squashy. While the eggs boil, make a roux of butter and flour, add the liquid from which you have lifted the chicory bundles, stir till the right consistency – just to coat the spoon; add top of milk, a little grated cheese if you like, for flavour and consistency, and pour over the chicory and the eggs with their anchovy fillets. If you want to keep it waiting, put a lid on, and leave it in the slow oven.

I see no point in par-boiling chicory to remove its slight bitterness – why eat a thing at all if you dislike its essential charactersitic? Better to offset it with something bland. But the difference between chicory cooked slowly or cooked quickly is very striking.

Another useful chicory dish is with ham; drain each cooked bundle, then roll in a thin slice of lean ham. Lay side by side in a clean dish, make a sauce from a butter-and-flour roux, use the liquid from the cooking dish, make up with milk or stock to a quantity just to cover the bundles – a lightish sauce, not a poultice; put on a lid and heat through. Chicory by itself is a good vegetable to serve with game pie, or roast duck, as well as, or instead of, brussels sprouts. It has enough character to survive with a rich and flavourful dish.

I can't understand people deprecating brussels sprouts, they must use poor, too-big, blowsy ones, or else overcook them. Reg now insists on growing only a Dutch seed, which its growers assure him is the only 'true' brussels sprout (another international confusion?), the others being imposters. I don't understand this, but he certainly grows perfect sprouts, small, neat, firm, delicate green outside and pink in the middle. They cook surprisingly quickly, it is essential to stop them when just tender enough to cut neatly in half – even a couple of minutes more and they start to go limp and are just a mess. Their delectable flavour is even more noticeable cold, tossed in a little olive oil with rock salt and fresh black pepper; no vinegar or lemon, but a sprinkle perhaps of fresh thyme – we have several thymes in the rockery which are evergreen. Or mixed with a few sliced mushrooms. They make quite an exciting dish if sprinkled with a little finely-chopped stem ginger and a very little garlic – those two flavourings so often paired in Chinese cookery! The sprouts must, of course, be the tiny tightly-closed ones.

Salsify (oyster plant) is a winter delicacy, though horrid to prepare, the spidery black roots look like some deep-sea monster. Verena is masterful with them – she knew all about salsify before I did, because a previous owner of this house grew it, and Verena, absurdly young, had worked for her, and told me how to cook and serve it. This too needs putting in lemony water till cooked, then par-boil it. I cut it into rounds or fingers according to the shape of the roots, then toss them in butter and parsley, which does full justice to the delicate flavour. But it is capable of more than this. It combines beautifully with scallops, and as these are so expensive now, makes them go further. While the salsify par-boils and the scallops cook in butter, I make a white sauce, pour a little into some big scallop shells I have, allowing two for each person, then slice scallops and salsify into each, sprinkling the coral on top, cover with the rest of the sauce, sprinkle with crumbs and some crumbled crispy bacon, dot with butter, then arrange the shells in a baking tin and put in to the hot oven. By the time we've had a drink, they will be brown and bubbling. Failing scallops, the invaluable tunny is a good substitute.

If there is enough celeriac to spare from soups and salads, it makes a lovely alternative to potatoes, boiled and mashed with butter and pepper and salt.

Towards the end of the month, January produces some gentle, mild days, deceptively spring-like. It is pleasant to be out in the afternoon sunshine looking to see if the coloured winter primroses are starting – which they would be if the birds hadn't pecked out the centre of each clump; I must cotton them. The green helle-bores already have their livid pale green flowerheads lifted above their beautiful dark green finger-like leaves, but they are not ready to pick yet; the individual bells have not formed and

separated. They have naturalized themselves all over the wild end of the garden, and the bright pale green clumps show from far away. Quite suddenly the first patches of aconites are showing colour, though the cups are still closed buttons above their frill of ferny green. With us the snowdrops generally come later, but after this hard winter they have come together. As always, the snowdrops spring up magically, overnight; they are not there, then they are. Massed on the bank above the stream, just opposite the house, they glimmer even after dusk, seeming to hold a light of their own. I pick some of both, the yellow and the white, for the vase on my dressing table. The first flowers of the new year – so we're off! Now the whole pageant of the year will roll on with overlapping waves of flowers to the year's end.

Reg says the village always reckons you can see to have tea without a light by the end of January. Village tea is at five-thirty when the men get home from work. When we no longer need to draw the curtains for tea, there always seems to be a blackbird on top of the rose-post outside the west window, singing towards the last of the sunset light.

# FEBRUARY

# FEBRUARY

'When Frost was spectre grey,
And winter's dregs made desolate
The weakening eye of day,
And all mankind that haunted nigh
Had sought their household fires.'

THOMAS HARDY

Something seems to have gone wrong with February. It ought to be a gentle month, a waiting-time between strong January and explosive March. But it isn't; it's a miserable time of slush and sneezes; the best time to be away. (But it is also the best working time! One has a sense of drawbridge up, no invaders.)

A few things decorate it. The aconites have become a golden sea. In our garden they definitely walk, coming up everywhere. They have completely covered the bank between the herb border and the further lawn, though this is as far as possible from the area under the nut tree where they were naturalized when we came (and they are rapidly filling in between). They come up all over the place, even between paving stones, and invade the borders. It doesn't really matter, because though one has to pull the leaves off in the end for tidiness, their tiny corms miraculously disappear, so they are not in the way of later plants. They are particularly lovely above a light fall of snow followed by sunshine; every yellow cup, surrounded by its feathery green, has a drop of water in it glittering like a diamond.

With the showers of yellow jasmine, flowering again after frosts, they are the sunshine of this dim and muted month. The snowdrops are really at the full now, single and double, a white drift beside the stream, and in the rockery, with clumps coming up in unexpected places. The hellebore is ready to pick, the sprays of pale green cups have separated and hang down, though the crimson rims haven't come yet – the warmth of the house may bring them out; they look lovely in copper bowls, surrounded by their own sharply contrasting dark green leaves, and they seem to last for ever. This English variety is called the Stinking Hellebore, because it has a slightly acrid smell when the thick soft stalk is cut, but this goes off before you've reached the house.

The coloured freesias have been brought up from the greenhouse to the study, and the pots stood in a row in the wide old fire embrasure; the mass of thin leaves need support, but the red and yellow and white and orange flowers on their wiry stems fill the room with their particularly delirious scent.

Some of the winter vegetables are beginning to fade out earlier than usual this year, No more celeriac, no more celery, the last of the sprouts. But the sorrel is coming on, small still, but a handful of the young leaves combine with chicory, mustard-and-cress, finely sliced leek and grated apple to make a mixed salad.

An exciting winter vegetable we can grow again, after many years when the tubers were unobtainable, is the Chinese artichoke. These are the length of my little finger and look like ivory corkscrews. They only need washing and brushing to get the soil off, then put them into bubbling butter, and cook till just tender, but firm and nutty, then sprinkle with parsley, chopped hard-boiled egg, crumbled crisp bacon; or just pepper and salt. I think they are best as a dish on their own, they look so pretty, and their texture is so important. Of course you can serve them as a vegetable with other dishes, in which case it might be better to boil or steam them, and give them a cheese or any other sauce; but I think this is a pity. Sown in the spring, they are ready in autumn and can be left in the ground and raised when wanted; Reg thinks it wiser to lift them when the soil is fairly dry and store them in sand – if only to avoid bringing them in clogged with wet earth.

The cabbages hanging in the woodshed are full of ice, but allowed to thaw out slowly they are perfect. The vivid red cabbages I shred finely on to a lump of butter melting in a fireproof dish, and layer with chopped onion and apple, then sprinkle with brown sugar (muscovado for choice), pepper and salt; most recipes include wine vinegar, but I think you want to go sparingly with this – just a desertspoonful, or it comes out too sharply acid; then as much red wine as you can spare, say a teacupful. Put a lid on and push to the back of the slow oven early in the afternoon, and it should be ready for dinner; turn it all over once or twice to mix and to keep the top part moist; taste to see when tender. Within reason, the longer it cooks the better, and it's said to improve with reheating, but we never seem to have any left. This is good served with thin slices of grilled ham on top as a main course.

I keep half-bottles of dry Spanish white wine and dry Spanish red, and a half-bottle of dry cider in the back of my fridge. Carefully corked they last extremely well, and are always available for the odd dish or sauce. Cider is a good substitute for champagne in many sauces or fruit recipes, and personally I'd rather drink the champagne.

The tight white cabbages I try to keep for coleslaw, but they are so good as a vegetable with rich dishes; like sprouts, they supply the contrasting freshness, almost as a salad does. I don't shred them, but tear the leaves apart and put them in a saucepan with a small cup of boiling water and a piece of butter or dripping and cook slowly, shaking the pan now and then. Watch to stop them as soon as they are tender. Steaming loses the colour and boiling loses the flavour (and goodness).

Even in February the skies clear sometimes, and there are still, sunny afternoons which bear no relation to the foggy mornings and frosty nights. On St Valentine's Day, a Sunday, the sun was warm, there was no wind, and everywhere the garden seemed coming to life. So Ralph announced he was going to open a bottle of Gaillac Perlé in the summerhouse at quarter-to-one sharp, thus declaring the season open. We have a large summerhouse, built in the 1920s by the gardener here – and very well built – of old bricks set herring-bone fashion in a frame of old oak timbers. It faces west, and for more than half the year we use it as another room. We took this first drink standing, because the chairs had been taken in for the winter and the space was filled by a garden-frame sheltering while its new glass settled in.

Ralph's winter heaths (erica carneas, because of the lime in our soil) are becoming beautiful, a thick, close-fitting coat of purple or white, clothing high stones in the rockery, or showing bright flickers of colour in sheltered corners. The yellow crocuses are beginning, making the aconites look pale. The buds are big on the daphnes, but not open yet. Two mallards swoop in, their usual beautiful flight down the stream, followed by a great splashing and a triumphant outburst of quacking, *Done it again! Got back to the water through all those trees without touching a twig!*

By teatime the sky was overcast, and that night there was a little snow. How can anyone ask why the English talk about the weather? It's the only country where it's worth talking about, because it's always changing, always surprising, always news. There is an old saying:

> If Candlemas be fair and bright,
> Winter will take another flight.

These country sayings are inescapably true, being the observation of many generations. This year Candlemas was fair and bright. . . ! Surely the snow can't come again? So many things have green buds, and the sap is rising in the roses. At least the thrushes are back, that must be a good sign? In summer, you can't walk about this garden without practically falling over thrushes. In a bad winter they disappear (gone to the woods for better grubs?), leaving the blackbirds to dominate, looking huge and black among the robins, bluetits, chaffinches, sparrows, an occasional flight of starlings. But today I saw a thrush.

There is always a mealtime to call me in from the garden, but my kitchen is a bright and welcoming place. When we came here there were two kitchens; Ralph soon redesigned them into one and took out four doors, two outer and two inner. Instead, he put in three more windows, two of them high up, which face south and bring in all possible light during the winter months; but by summer the sun is higher and has moved round further, so misses them and never makes it too hot. In full summer it is through the original windows on the north side that the sun shines – too late to be hot, just glinting pinkly at evening. So it is pleasant all the year round. One of the old doors had been a 'maid's entrance' to a narrow outside passage; Ralph brought this into the kitchen with its charming red-tiled roof, and took out the plaster panels of the dividing wall, leaving the oak studs to stand as a screen. The Aga nestles into the embrasure where the coal range must once have stood, and a fridge fits into an alcove where there used to be another door. The centre of the room is clear – room for large dogs, large trugs of vegetables and whoever is carrying them. The floor is goldeny straw matting over old bricks. The line of cupboards on either side of the Aga were made on the spot by Kenneth, our favourite carpenter, who practically lived with us at one time; he used natural oak. The formica on top is raspberry red, the paint of the two remaining doors, the surround of the new windows and the cupboards under the sink (in what had been a separate room, and is narrower than the main room), is a strong kingcup yellow. Between the studs of dark wood, the plaster panels of the walls and the surprisingly high irregular ceiling are cream gloss paint.

We found a high-backed settle – pine with an oak seat, a late-eighteenth-century import from the North American colonies I should think. We had it in the hall at first, but when Ralph re-designed the kitchen we felt that was its proper place. It fits in perfectly, and I asked Kenneth to make me a little oak bookshelf for my cook books; this hangs beside the settle, so I can sit there to look up recipes and plan menus – my Elizabeth David paper-backs are falling to pieces, I must really replace them; in all the books I use old restaurant cards as book-markers, evoking memories of happy meals in far places.

I am getting down to the root vegetables in February, but still no problem about soups. Ordinary Jerusalem artichokes are still there. Parsnips, as well as being useful for soup, are good if par-boiled, baked or fried with butter or dripping till slightly crusty, and mixed with sliced mushrooms. There are still leeks, and the chicory is going strong. We have finished the gourds, alas! but still have some Chinese artichokes, and I must not forget the huge, sweet onions.

Reg has prepared five-foot rows for lettuces, sowing just a little patch at a time, so there will be a sequence; he puts cloches over the rows to warm the soil in advance. Under cloches he has sown spring onion, carrot and radish. In the greenhouse, a box of broad beans (Green Windsor), and a box of globe artichokes, in case of winter losses, and because it's better to renew them every few years.

The nicest part of a February day is the evening, I think. My cooking time is very cosy, with Yiwara by the Aga, Ralph down in the study. Often I even fail to hear the telephone; it is a secluded, peaceful time. Ralph gauges when I shall be about ready, and comes up to the house. Yiwara moves to the hall, thus being in touch with both of us, in accordance with her built-in guarding, sheepdog instinct. When our meal is ready and I've laid the table, I go upstairs and change (only to another pair of pants and a different shirt, but it is more relaxed and refreshing for the evening). Then I throw off all the work and responsibilities of the day, and go into the drawing-room. Yiwara jumps up from the hall and comes with me. Ralph may have brought some work up to finish, but now he pushes it away. He has a bottle of wine standing at the end of the fireplace, and two glasses warming on the mantelpiece. Ash logs are piled on the fire, and Yiwara stretches in front of it, her coat mingling with the fur of the rug – full-length she nearly stretches from end to end. Here is comfort and brightness and peace. February is shut out.

# MARCH

# MARCH

'. . . daffodils,
That come before the swallow dares and take
The winds of March with beauty.'

SHAKESPEARE

It's curious how often the feel and look of the weather changes quite sharply with our arbitrary naming of the months. Even as early as 2 March, the day couldn't be anything but March. Bright and bitter, a blue sky with a few fluffy white clouds skimming across it, everything in the garden moving, moving, with the erratic swirling wind.

The birds have gone blowsy and floppy, flapping their wings in voluptuous anticipation of the spring. Some are even mating, or pretending to, and so are the ducks on the stream. The daffodil and narcissus green has shot up and become a thicket; the yellow crocuses edging the border along the drive open wide to the sun and are shining orange. Unexpected pockets of the garden are stirring to life. It is the suddenness with which things emerge that makes March exciting: the thick green points of the chives are up, a fringe along the front of the herb border, taller every day, they are ready to start cutting. The lettuces under cloches are big now, and the lamb's lettuce is still good; the sorrel has roared up and the leaves are now big enough to cook. Going across the stream to pick it, I look with reviving interest at the fruit cage, with the raspberry canes tied in for the new season beginning to leaf, and the neat rows of strawberry plants. The swamp cypress we planted on the bank long ago (because we'd read it likes to have its toes in the water) is just showing bronzy tips of new growth.

So much sorrel must be picked to make anything when cooked. I press the leaves down in the piled colander to take back to the kitchen. Today we can have the first sorrel soup. I pull the washed leaves off the central vein and pile them on to a lump of butter in a saucepan, then leave them on a slow heat to melt. Very soon they are a soft dark green mess – so little to show for the original mountain of leaves! At first I eke out the sorrel with a little potato and onion cooked separately, then emulsified together and brought to the quantity and thickness I desire with stock – the flavour of the sorrel will always dominate. But my favourite sorrel soup – the real, special sorrel soup! – is only possible when the leaves are big enough to make sufficient quantity by themselves. Then it needs a huge saucepan to hold the raw leaves and melt them over butter; there's never enough at the end, never as much as you had expected. I add boiled milk to the melted sorrel. It curdles into white strings, but do not despair. Put it through the liquidizer and all signs of curdling vanish as if by magic and leave a smooth pale green purée. Then add more milk to make it the thickness of cream. Somehow the milk offsets the sharp tang of the sorrel. Add cream and, for perfection, an egg yolk or two beaten into the cream (add a little hot soup to this, then incorporate it into the main quantity, but do not let it boil). Sprinkle with chopped chives, hard-boiled egg or shrimps; or an island of stiff cream in the middle with shrimps in it. This is also a lovely cold soup when the weather makes such an idea attractive.

Sorrel, melted over butter, is a delicious filling for an omelette – again, the sharp flavour offsets the blandness of the eggs. Just lift the dark green lump of hot sorrel out of its liquid and spread it over the centre of the half-set omelette, then fold the sides over.

The chicory clamp must be cleared during March, before it starts sprouting through the soil and turning green. But throughout this month it is a wonderful standby, cooked or raw. Astonishingly, there are still lovely little sprouts.

The Aura potatoes are still perfect. This intriguing, invaluable and little-known potato was developed by Lord Antrim in Ireland, experimenting with a French stock. In effect, he has achieved a 'new' potato all the year round, because it is a maincrop, and lasts. Waxy and yellow, kidney-shaped, it is perfect for anything except squashing with a good sauce – it won't squash; we use the last of the Majestic for this. But if you toss them in butter and grate parsley over them, you can pass them off as new potatoes during the most improbable months, if you wish. I think it's more fun to tell people, and offer your friends some for seed. We have dotted Suffolk with Aura potatoes, and even taken some further afield. Ah, the things that travel in spongebags, or in the toes of shoes!

Another winter vegetable still holding out is leeks, so one can make vichyssoise, but a hot vichyssoise seems ruined to me, and in cold weather the point of a soup is to warm you, so . . . a delicious hot leek soup with cheese grated on it. The leeks are big now; I cut them in inch-chunks and steam them till barely tender, drain them, put them in a fireproof dish and cover them with a tunny sauce – a white sauce with drained tunny flaked into it. To sprinkle with coarsely-ground nuts – walnut or hazel – makes a nice contrast of texture. Coarsely chopped hard-boiled egg in the sauce instead of tunny is an alternative; sprinkle with breadcrumbs and grated cheese and brown under grill (or in top of Aga).

Why is it always so cold when I prune the roses? I work determinedly along the four beds of hybrid tea roses running down from the house towards the stream, head down, scarf blowing off; then along the four arms of floribundas which run left and right on either side. These were filled, when we first came, with big fluffy heads of Polyantha roses, as they used to be called, in a bluish-pink somehow right for an old garden. But when some died, and I tried to replace them, a nurseryman told me he didn't know their name, that they had passed from the commercial market, and I should only 'find them in another old garden'. So Reg is raising some from cuttings. I tried unsuccessfully to fill the gaps with other pink floribundas which looked quite wrong, then I discovered a new one called 'Yesterday' in the same mauve-ish pink, with big trusses of tiny flowers, which is perfect. This first pruning day the wind was bitter, and I raced on scarcely raising my head.

The next day, miraculously, spring came, and the world was a different place. It didn't last, but for a day there was a softness in the air, the sun was warm, there was no wind. I heard the frogs croaking, always the harbinger of spring with us. We used to think they came down the stream and turned into our lily ponds to spawn; then one year Reg drained the ponds, and found them all hibernating in the mud at the bottom. The lumps of jelly spawn are not attractive – but they come with the early daffodils opening, with the young foliage of the willows almost as golden as the

forsythias, with the violets flowering in scented mats everywhere, pink and blue and white in any uncultivated corner. A patch has somehow established itself in a corner of one of the rose beds round the sundial. Of course they shouldn't be there, but they are so pretty, the three colours have mixed themselves, and the scent is wonderful as I prune the floribundas. The deep continuous croaking of the frogs in the ponds is a part of this season. But I do wish they wouldn't cross the garden and copulate outside the kitchen door.

Today there is that strange lethargy which comes in the midst of all the activity of spring, a slack yielding to the sudden warmth, a surrender to the caressing day. All the birds are singing to claim the places where they intend to build, and Yiwara lies stretched out on the little lawn in front of the summerhouse as if it were full summer.

There is a great friendliness in a familiar garden. Plants you have forgotten since last year arrive again. I once put a handful of pale stripey crocuses between the paving stones opposite the dining-room window, and there they are, several flowers to a bulb now. But the species crocus I had put in the grass beside them to

come earlier have all vanished – eaten by field mice? The earliest erythroniams (dog's-tooth violets, so called because their white roots are the shape of a dog's tooth) have erupted in a corner of the border. They are dainty little pinky-mauve flowers with speckled leaves, and however often the border is dug over, they survive, never more, never less, in exactly the same place. The most colourful part of the garden at the moment is Ralph's rockery, especially the deep sloping corner opposite the house. It is brilliant with a carpet of white and purple heaths and a bright blue sea of chionodoxas and scillas, sky-blue and white, radiant, with some fluffy pale blue puschkinias at the top of the steps. The rose beds are edged with hyacinths. These are my winter house bulbs of many years, they seem to go on and on, never diminishing in size – benefiting from the manure given to the rose beds probably. A line of pink face a line of blue nearest the house, then white on both sides running down to the path above the stream. I changed them over when I saw how long the white ones showed after dusk when the coloured ones had vanished; two thick lines of brilliant white, and beyond them the white of the ducks asleep on the further bank.

March is the month of sowing. I make my lists and order seeds sitting by the winter's fire, and it is always exciting when they arrive. Just that little cardboard box! and from it will come all the thick high green rows of vegetables, all the loaded summer baskets brought into the kitchen, to be cooked when the sun is so far round it shines in redly through the north window, and we eat late because the lovely day fades so slowly.

Only a few root vegetables hang on to bridge the gap between last year and this; potatoes, onions, carrots, parsnips, artichokes. I have only just discovered that Reg actually uses a notebook I gave him three years ago to record the dates of sowing, time of germination, and date of cropping. Ralph had said, 'He'll never bother to write it down. He carries it in his head, which is much better.' And indeed he has a fantastic memory for the dates of sowing and harvesting various crops, comparing them over different years, relating early and late, fast and slow, to the weather of that particular season. This is the real gardening lore.

But he uses my book! I have just been shown it. I remember

him coming back over the bridge from a day's digging with a tired, but happy smile, saying, 'Oh, the soil's working beautifully today! Fine, just dry enough, just damp enough – warm, like summer! Just what you want!' It is very unusual for a gardener to find everything just right; he must have gauged the one day when it was. But though I had chosen the seeds and ought to have known, even I was impressed at the long list in his book.

GREENHOUSE
Petunia
Cabbage Winter White
Brussels True
Autumn cauliflower
Cabbage Early Red King
Tomato
Capsicum
Aubergine
Celery, White and Red
Celeriac

OUTSIDE
Peas, Onward
Potatoes, early
Every ten to fourteen days: spring
    onions, carrot, radish, lettuce
Leek seed
Onion seed
Shallots
Jerusalem artichoke
Carrot
Parsnip
Sweet peas

Already, under rows of cloches, there are autumn-sown peas a foot high, sweet peas up several inches, a row of really good lettuces with nice hearts, and a younger row coming on. The herbs are putting out new green, the fennel very bright and fluffy. In the greenhouse, seed boxes need watching to snatch off the glass and paper the moment they have germinated. The azaleas are showing colour and can come up to the house.

At the end of March the clocks go forward to Summer Time. Suddenly the evenings are light, and life begins to change. The cosy, locked-in, secret time is over, when one could lose oneself in work. Now the drawbridge must go down. Foreign publishers arrive like swallows – Swedish, German, American, French, Dutch. We instinctively start planning some travel, as everything is on the move. I cook the last Christmas pudding. More daffodils come out every day, along by the stream, on the bank under the cherry trees, in clumps at the back of the border. No other flower so lights the garden with a sunshine of its own, whatever the weather. Morning after morning they are all pinched and white and bent with frost, sometimes a whole sheaf with their heads bowed to the ground. But as the sun reaches them, miraculously (you never actually catch them moving) they will stand up, open, expand, radiant again and faintly stirring.

# APRIL

# APRIL

'. . . but the quarry that he made
Whenever April comes as it came in old time,
Is a dear delight to the man who loves a maid
For the primrose comes from the lime . . .

And the blackbird builds below the catkin shaking,
And the sweet white violets are beauty in the blood,
And daffodils are there, and the blackthorn blossom breaking
Is a wild white beauty in bud.'

JOHN MASEFIELD

So many contradictory things are said about April! A great priest said, 'Whoever understands the meaning of the word April, understands the meaning of the word resurrection.' But T. S. Eliot called April 'the cruellest month'. Who said it is the month 'when the earth opens to receive the seed'?

One falls in love with other months for a general impression of lovely days, but April is the maverick, changeling, provocative month, with black clouds racing up the sky while dazzling sunshine still makes the young green treetops look golden against them. Then straight rods of glittering rain drive coldly over the massed daffodils and flowering bushes, and a minute later the sun reasserts itself and makes all the raindrops sparkle. April has the fascination of difficult people, who are often the most attractive – what will they do next?

Infinitely variable, April may suddenly spread a deceptively gentle enchantment; a mist of green softens the whole country, and, with us a blue mist of grape hyacinths under the daffodils and in pools of deep blue all over the garden, blurred to a stain of colour; they are one of the things that naturalize uncontrollably here.

Loveliest of trees, the cherry now
Is hung with bloom along the bough . . .

No other blossom is in the least like the cherry. Dainty, fluttering, a fairie tree; and at night it is alive, moving imperceptibly, a happy ghost of a tree.

We have two enormous 'real' cherries, fruiting as distinct from decorative, between sixty and sixty-five feet high. From the house, and from most parts of the garden, you see one behind the other, so they make a single mountain of blossom, their supple black branches sweeping very wide. They show no hint of green till their flowers are nearly over and most of the blossom is strewn on the lawn (cherries vary in this, I've noticed). As you go upstairs, they fill our bedroom window which faces you.

April 23rd always seems a magic date to me – the cherry and the cuckoo and the nightingales have all arrived. Shakespeare's birthday, St George's Day; the date I first noticed, because I went to my first real ball wearing my first real ball gown; the day on which, for six years, we flew from England to Malta to sail *Mary Deare* in the Eastern Mediterranean, and I could hardly bear to leave the burgeoning garden, knowing I should not see it again till the late roses in mid-July. Always I am torn between wanting to go and wanting to stay, between excitement and security. I used to go and stand under the great cherries the last night, and looking up through layer upon layer of blossom to see the moon was like looking up through soapsuds.

Although they are so big, and I believe so old, they bear excellent cherries, a red crossed with the famous Polstead Black (the cherry which has been exported to start orchards all over the world). It's impossible to protect them from the birds, but in a good year, when the frost hasn't nipped them, there are enough for everyone; in a bad year we don't even try any more. Ralph wrote *The White South* sitting under the cherry trees pulling as often as he thought of it at a contraption we had rigged up to scare the birds – a nice contrast to the snowy Antarctic waste he was writing about! When we have enough, we make a Black Cherry Preserve from this Swiss recipe:

Stone the cherries (you can buy a little gadget for this, which is also useful for olives). If they are ripe and sweet, you only need half a pound of sugar to each pound of fruit. Put the sugar with a couple of tablespoons of water in a pan and stir over a low heat

until it froths. Then put in the cherries and let them bubble on a low heat for about ten minutes, skimming off the froth. Remove from fire and strain through a sieve, letting them drain well. Boil up the syrup with the juice in it until it thickens again, then return the cherries to it for about fifteen minutes and let them bubble gently till the syrup is thick enough 'to pour off the spoon in ribbons'. Pour into a shallow bowl and leave till next day, then bottle cold – if bottled hot the cherries will rise to the top.

This gives you whole cherries of fresh flavour in a thick dark syrup, the consistency to eat with a spoon, as preserves are eaten in Norway – not set. It is lovely with junket, or over home-made ice-cream; over melon, or pears, or peaches or bananas, or a mixed fruit salad; or with any fairly sharp cream cheese.

Our most spectacular cherry tree is Tai Haku, with huge white blossoms, and leaves that are pinkish when young. She spreads into an umbrella shape, and stands on the opposite side of the lawn from the fruiting cherries, about half their height. From the west window in the drawing-room we look along a bank between lawn and hedge which we have planted with alternating patches of early yellow daffodils and late white narcissi. Looking along the length of this bank, over the white narcissi to the towering white cherries, with the westering sun beyond, is one of the prettiest sights of the garden's year.

The willows are fluffier every day, a delicate lime-yellow. The sweetbriar leaves are open enough to smell delicious after rain. The pink japonicas are in flower now, along the walls of the house and in the bushes opposite – a wonderful shrub for soil too limey to grow hydrangeas or azaleas! The mahonias are covered with their brilliant yellow head of tiny flowers, and they, too, seem everywhere. Both these shrubs were here before we were, and though I'm not sure I would have chosen them, they are a part of the garden to me and I have become fond of them. The coloured primroses are at the full – dark blue, light blue, crimson, pink, purple, yellow, white. These I grow from seed, and plant in a little bed near the front door, and along the south wall of the summer-house. And in the corner of the border nearest the house I have put a clump of exquisite white erythroniums, like little lilies. I have never seen this variety advertised. We bought ours long ago from a wild 'small' grower in Ireland. He specialized in unusual plants, and his roughly-typed list was lyrical ('You'll scarcely sleep at nights for thinking of these delicate beauties out in the rough weather'). Then that great gardener V. Sackville-West discovered him, and wrote a column about him. So postmen began to arrive with sacks of orders . . . it was too much for him, he just couldn't cope, so he had a drink, sold up at cut prices, and went out of business. Our garden is sprinkled with things we bought from that last desperate, untidy list of treasures, but we mourned his passing. The blue wood anemones that now form a solid carpet between the daffodils in a little dell above the stream, behind the two big yews, came from him.

On either side of the front door, wallflowers fill two handsome square brick containers which Ralph built in early days, to give more character to our solid plain oak door. Wallflowers too on either side of the summerhouse, wafting scent as you pass, the first scent of the year! and so many, many different colours.

The greenhouse is fuller than ever of seed boxes neatly covered to germinate, and the seed propagator is full. The woody stalks of the fuschias are breaking out with new leaves, the begonias are sprouting, and the dahlias. Stalwart tomato plants are getting quite tall.

Reg has a big planting list this month.

| IN THE GREENHOUSE | Cucumber (Landora) |
| | Melon |
| | Tomato |
| | Sweetcorn (first early) |
| | Marrow |
| | Nicotiana (tobacco plant) |
| | Stock (ten-week) |
| | Polyantha |
| | Cineraria |
| | Ipomoea (morning glory) |
| | |
| OUTSIDE | Peas (Lord Chancellor) |
| | Broad beans from greenhouse put under cloche |
| | Broad beans (Long pod, sown outside) |
| | Main crop potatoes |
| | Peas |

Dwarf beans (Masterpiece)
Lettuce (ten-fourteen days interval)
Radish
Spring onion (White Lisbon)
Carrot

Now the beech trees in our woods are advanced enough to open in water, so I can cut branches and start the copper jug at the bend of the stairs. Our staircase, which comes down into the centre of the hall, has finely-carved twisted banisters on both sides, 'frog banisters'. When we opened up the hall, we tried to get some more made, but no modern carpenter dared cut so deeply for fear of going right through; it is just the deep rounded hollows of the old ones that give them their fragile grace. The small landing between the two flights is a central vantage point, seen from upstairs, downstairs, when you come in the front door, wherever you move about the house. I keep flowers and branches there all the year, starting with the beech leaves – branches taller than I am, with sprays pushing through the banisters and lying over the handrail. When I give a party, I feel that one the pitcher on the stairs is done, the situation is in hand and there's really not much left to worry about.

This time of year I stand in the kitchen wondering what to cook. The last of the old vegetables are the onions. One uses onions all the time as flavouring, but it's worth remembering they can be delicious on their own. I like to cook these big sweet onions in their skins (but using an old saucepan, as their strong brown dye stains). When tender enough to prod with a fork, drain them, and as soon as cool enough to handle, cut off top and bottom skin and outer leaves. They are a nice base to an egg fricassée, and make it more substantial. I cut each onion – one for each person – into three or four thick soft slices, and arrange them in the bottom of a fireproof dish. On top of them I put hard-boiled eggs sliced longways, and cover with a white sauce, béchamel or velouté, depending on whether you want to use milk or stock. Sprinkle with fine breadcrumbs and grated cheese, dot with butter, and put in the hot oven till it is brown and bubbling. Or use fillets of plain white fish in place of eggs.

Cauliflowers are not one of our most successful crops, but when there is a good one, I make a dish I learned in Norway. A newly-met Norwegian friend took us in his speed-boat to his holiday island. I think he was very proud of this vicious vessel, and wanted to show its paces; he went at such a wild speed, jerking the tiller to avoid bits of land or other boats at the very last minute. That ride is indelibly linked in my mind with the dish he served us. 'This is a Norwegian dish', he said.

Put the lightly-cooked cauliflower whole, tender but firm, in a fireproof dish, then throw prawns over it – a lot of prawns, this is not a garnish, but the main food; shrimps will do, but there must be enough. Then squeeze lemon juice over them, and pour melted butter over with whatever herb you choose, fennel or marjoram or lemon balm. We ate it that night with a creamy white sauce, but I think I like lemon and melted butter better.

Reg is bringing in the young rhubarb, which I cook with brown sugar and a squeeze of lemon, no water. And suddenly the asparagus is ready! We have a very selfish asparagus bed, only enough for ourselves. It was here when we came, and despising it, we started a new one. This never worked. Perhaps we hadn't realized how much goodness was drained away by the willow roots, or how far they stretched. So we abandoned it, and went back to cherishing the old one. I read somewhere that you should run not walk to the kitchen when you've cut asparagus. Of course this is the delicate green asparagus of English gardens, not the thick white or purple kind grown commercially, which has so much less flavour.

I still have some bottles of gooseberries on the larder shelf to make gooseberry fool (enough cream and not too much sugar – tangy), and some jars of black currant purée for sorbets. I have the last of Verena's bottled tomatoes to make a sauce for pasta, and her fresh, fresh tasting jams, strawberry and raspberry, lovely to spread in the light crisp sandwich cakes she bakes for tea.

There is a lot of sorrel, good lettuces, young radishes; the garden is still feeding us, with the last of the old and the first of the new.

When the sorrel leaves are big enough, but young and bright green, they can be the base of a quite substantial salad, a light main course. Pick enough to make a mound on everybody's plate, wash and tear out the stalk and main vein, and tear into pieces. Combine with coarsely chopped hard-boiled egg, at least one for each person;

finely chopped onion, crisply fried thin rashers of bacon, blotted on kitchen paper to remove grease, and roughly broken. Make enough of your usual vinaigrette to coat lightly the salad you have made, then stir into it a little curry paste (it dissolves better than powder). Add a little good stock, chicken or guinea fowl or duck, in proportion of one tablespoon to three of vinaigrette; heat this, stirring, then pour the hot dressing over the salad at the last moment before eating. This heats but does not cook the ingredients, and the warmth brings out all the flavours. Diced cold chicken or flaked firm white cooked fish, or finely sliced mozzarella cheese could be added. Spinach could be substituted for the sorrel, but is not so tender when raw.

Some days are warm enough to sit out, and temptingly bright – choosing whichever seat is most sheltered, and looking along the whole length of the stream thickly fringed with daffodils. We have more of the later creamy ones than of the first brilliant yellow, so the colour is softer now than last month, and the clumps thicker. Ralph's father gave us a very good collection when we first came here (none of us knew what was already in the garden) and they have increased and multiplied over the years; so many varieties, including the scented poeticus narcissi. The hyacinths edging the rose beds are still full and brilliant.

But spring comes late in Suffolk, compensated for by our long golden autumn. I cut a poem called *Blackthorn Winter*, by Joyce Westrup, out of a newspaper once, and stuck it in the back of an anthology. I love it because it is so true for us, where the blackthorn stays white in the hedges for so long, waiting till the east wind stops at last, and with the first warm sun the flowers are drowned in their own green leaves.

> The ice-thin wind blows keen to freeze
> The timid blossom on the trees;
> How can it spare a thing so frail
> As this soft-feathered nightingale?
>
> Her song enchants the bitter air.
> With all desire and all despair.
> Unharboured from the frozen moon
> She sings grim April into June.

# MAY

# MAY

'The day was too bright for death. It was
a stainless day.'

                                        A. E. COPPARD

'The young May moon is bright, my love.'

'**M**ay is the month one has to be at home to deal with
the weeds,' Ralph says. 'No gardener can afford
to be away in May.'

Weeds are very racist in my flower borders –
no integration at all. My white border, which runs in three sections
across the garden from drive to river, is the haunt of bindweed.
Reg once dug it out to a depth of several feet, but it came merrily
up next year. The coloured herbaceous border beside the drive
from house to gate is bedevilled by ground elder. Ralph's rockeries
on the other side of the drive have both, also grass which grows
actually on top of the cushions of flowers, but pulls out easily after
rain (which is when the midges are worst, of course). Reg has never
taken against weeds, not really. He regards them as a part of nature
one just has to live with; they don't bother him.

But May, the most advertised month for going almost anywhere, is so beautiful at home one doesn't want to miss it. We did
miss it, for the six years we were sailing *Mary Deare* in the Eastern
Mediterranean. May and June are the best months for sailing in
the Aegean, as it's too cold earlier, and from July the meltemi is
too strong for pleasant sailing. Our first year home, I was excited
almost to tears by the radiance of England when the grass is that
unbelievable green, the cow parsley and the hawthorns are foaming
everywhere, the buttercups are out in the fields and the bluebells in
the woods. I've seen spring in other countries, uncurling while you
watch in its haste to become summer, but nowhere else that extra-

ordinary glory of light and colour as if the world had just been made, new-minted, and everything must stop and stare, as at a miracle. Dylan Thomas says:

> . . . it was all
> Shining, it was Adam and maiden,
> The sky gathered again
> And the sun grew round that very day.
> So it must have been after the birth of the simple light
> In the first, spinning place, the spellbound horses walking warm,
> Out of the whinnying green stable
> On to the fields of praise.

This must be the England of the exiles' memories, that aching nostalgia which is soaked through our literature; people parched and shrivelling in countries where the sun is a torment, remembering this moist green land. Flecker speaks for them:

> Meadows of England shining in the rain
> Spread wide your daisied lawns
> Till my far morning.

There are mornings of white mist which becomes luminous as the sun permeates it, and it thins like a veil withdrawing from some magic secret.

In our garden, the dominant tree in early May is a dark pink Malus, long sprays massed with purplish buds opening to single flowers, the leaves red. It is a great ball of dusky pink, taking the eye as the cherries disappear into green. At the end of the drive, we have a double white lilac in the angle of the old red brick wall, and on the other side of the gate a dark double purple, with a laburnum showering above it. These three trees are really large now, it's difficult to remember we planted them!

The white lilac I discovered at the far end of the garden, and came running to say, 'We've got a double white lilac down by the bridge, but it's no good there – it's enormous, it's buried, and it's only got one spray of flowers way out of reach, just to show what it is.' So Ralph cut out all the big branches, dug it up and moved it to this corner with just a few shoots of less than my height. Now it is a landmark every spring, covered with sculptured heads of fat, heavy, scented blossom. The dark purple lilac in a corner of the lawn on the other side of the drive, my mother brought us. She'd admired one in a stranger's garden just before she came to live with us, and the owner broke off two pieces and said, 'Dig a hole for each, put them in with a whole bucket of water, fill it up with earth and just leave it.' We did exactly that, and now each has made an enormous tree, flowering every year with rich exuberance. (The other is at the end of my white border – I didn't know then that I was going to make it a white border.)

The laburnum showering down above the dark lilac by the gate, and glinting through it, is a Vossii; we bought this variety for its long, heavy racemes. Now we have to cut it back, because it hangs over the gate. This group of purple and white and gold is an explosion of colour in May, all the rest of the year they withdraw into quiet green. There's an old red may tree behind, and greeny-white guelder roses beginning. The vivid bluish-pink of the rock phlox in the rockery echoes the lilac, so do a variety of aubretias, and a few tulips, and the purple flower of the honesty which sows itself in odd corners. The garden has become purple, last month it was yellow. It all seems right for this exuberant month, shouting with life.

At the far end of the garden, beyond the house, under the walnut tree, the species rose Canarybird is covered with butter-yellow single flowers like butterflies – the first of the roses, a May rose. The very old walnut tree is at last putting forth its leaves, always the last to green. The swifts have come, darting through the middle-air after insects, they are so fast and strong one ducks if they come too near, hearing the swish of their wings. Then the swallows come, sharp black silhouettes. The cuckoo calls against the background cooing of doves, and the blackbirds will sit on the very tip of clipped bushes, looking most heraldic, but wearing them bald with the clamping of their feet. The willows are changing from young gold to their summer silvery-green.

I had always missed out on tulips, because during our sailing years we were away when they would have been in flower. Then Ralph's Dutch publishers sent us home from a visit to them with a splendid consignment of bulbs. He planted them in groups in the corners of the four beds round the sundial, so now these brilliant colours suddenly splash out, still unfamiliar and surprising.

A day comes in May when it is warmer out than in, and the front door stands open. It is not really the 'front' door, but the garden door, and when we came it opened into a passage. The real front door is on the opposite side of the house, and opens into the far end of the small original hall beside the drawing-room door. But the prettiest way of coming to the house was obviously through the beautiful wrought-iron gates (said to have come from Woburn, and to have been given a special dispensation during the war when metal gates were melted down) then up the drive through the garden.

So after a few years, when we'd dealt with more urgent things, and had time to think, we decided to open up the centre of the house. Basically, its structure is very simple. A hall with rooms opening off it, and upstairs a 'frog' banistered gallery with bedrooms leading off. But the whole effect of this lovely hall had been destroyed; at some time a large square room panelled in plywood had been partitioned out of it, the brick walls transforming the hall into a narrow brick-floored passage leading under the staircase to a small area containing the old front door, a magnificent iron spit built into the far end, and half the staircase. And we hated the blank-walled entrance from the garden door.

I'd expected the brick walls would come down easily, but make a lot of dust. Quite the contrary; they had to be practically unpicked, brick by brick, and made no dust. A Suffolk builder, Mr Kingsbury, Senior, who understood old houses, undertook the job. His family had been builders hereabouts for generations, he told us. He had the firm's pay-books back for two hundred years, and knew they went back further; but at that date the family had divided, one brother going to America, and the records were lost. We called him the Master Builder. He put in steel girders to take the weight when the brick walls came down, but the timber-framed structure of the house was itself as strong as an iron frame. The function of the new girders was to support the upstairs floors and walls and to act as ties against the danger of lateral thrust on the exterior wall framing.

The transformation of the house when cleared to its original timber-framed structure was overwhelming. The big square room, the passage beside it, the small hall at the end, were now all one, divided two-thirds/one-third by what we could now see and appreciate for the first time as a very fine staircase. The Master Builder's best carpenter copied the frog banisters, curved hand-rail and twisted corner-post for the side of the staircase which had been bricked in, so it was now opened out and symmetrical. He was a very good carpenter, but even he could not 'turn' the wood – carve the twist as deeply – as his ancestors had done, for fear of going right through. Now for the first time we could enjoy the original hall. With three big windows on the south side, and one on the north, the sun shone right through. The old front door was at the diagonally opposite corner from the garden door; the drawing-room, dining-room, and what is now my sitting-room open off it. It became the natural centre of the whole house, upstairs as well as downstairs, giving a feeling of light and space.

How to find a carpet (that we could afford) big enough for its not-too-good wooden floor – even for the ex-morning-room part, leaving the passage and old hall with their faded pinky bricks? Then we read a sale notice in the local paper and rushed off, taking with us a friend we'd invited to come sailing with us – we had a little estuary boat at the time. He arrived suitably dressed, and was puzzled at our going off to bid for a carpet – thought he must have got the invitation spelt wrong. We found a dear old Turkish carpet, saw the colour, tawny, was right, and didn't even unfold it. When we got it home we spread it on the terrace to beat the dust out of it, and found it in good condition except for a hole in one corner, which we put a piece of furniture over. We were very happy with that carpet for many years – until we bought our present one, a lovely rose and silvery-green, 'old' in the right sense, from the Vigo Street Galleries.

So now when summer comes, and the garden door is opened in the morning and closed at night, there seems little division between in and out, and Yiwara drapes herself over the step to make the point.

The vegetable garden burgeons with promise, and the first of the new season's crops creep up on one, always a surprise. Delicious young radishes, round and scarlet, tiny carrots, young spring onions. But I'm still glad to fall back on sprouting broccoli; their tops, the hard stalks discarded, cook very quickly; their flavour and texture better when steamed, but the colour remains brighter if plunged into boiling water for a few minutes. Butter and pepper and salt are enough, but I discovered some of our nuts from last year still moist and firm; stored in a biscuit tin in their husks, and left on the stone floor of the larder. I put some through a coarse mill and sprinkled over the broccoli.

The lettuces are really fine now, with big hearts. Though my sorrel is running to flower, I still pick some of the youngest leaves to mix with lettuce; I like the contrasts of light and dark green, and of sharp and bland flavours; then chopped chives and (or) grated lemon balm, which is also with us again and gives a delicate lemony flavour to so many dishes.

The watercress is beginning in the lily pools; we have to restrict this rampant grower to the smallest, least obvious pool. They are fed by a stream running under the house – or rather, running under the gap between the house and the study. Infuriatingly, we've failed to naturalize it in the main stream. As well as salads, when it really gets going in quantity it makes lovely soup. I use my usual base of a few old potatoes (worth saving some for this purpose) and an onion simmered in a light stock till tender, then liquidized; meanwhile, wash and pick over enough watercress to fill (not just decorate!) the soup when it is finely chopped or put through the herb mill. Add cream or top of milk and seasoning and a squeeze of lemon juice. If served hot, a few shrimps in each dish look pretty, but if to serve cold, I put a few apples – any still surviving which are firm – peeled and cored and added to the liquidizer, with one, coarsely chopped, sprinkled on top as a garnish.

By the end of May the first peas are ready under the cloches – delectable! Friends who have been unable to escape frozen peas have asked what they were. 'Just green peas', we said. 'Yes, but they're some special variety, surely?' 'No, they've just been picked, that's all.'

A row of cauliflowers is ready now. Oddly enough, they always seem to me a winter vegetable, but they make a delicious extra salad. The flowerets need only the briefest cooking and must be quite firm, then anointed while warm with a dressing of oil and vinegar, salt, pepper and French mustard and chopped marjoram (which is now well up in the herb border). A few capers sprinkled over the dish go well, or finely cut fillets of anchovy, with a border of mustard-and-cress. The flowerets, raw, are good dipped into sour cream with French mustard stirred into it. A whisper, no more, of garlic is good in the salad dressing, but not enough to compete with the delicate flavour. Alternatively, take the white head of a young cauliflower and leave for a few minutes in salted water. Then shake, sprinkle with nutmeg and a little salt and pepper, and immerse in boiling stock – leave till the stalks are tender – cut off any that won't soften. It looks pretty served whole. If you have a lot of tiny cauliflowers, serve one to each person, surrounded with watercress.

I hope to escape from soup-making in the summer, but cannot resist sometimes making cold ones. If I can spare enough cauliflowers, I like this cold, and it's so simple; just simmer (only the white part) in a light stock, and liquidize in enough liquid to make it thick and creamy, then thin to the consistency you like with top of milk or cream, add pepper and salt and nutmeg. Sprinkle with finely chopped chives, then with very coarsely chopped black olives. With cold soups I always serve hot oatcakes.

Our selfish asparagus bed is worth visiting every other night. I find the punnets of an old pressure cooker are perfect to cook it in, as they keep the heads standing above the water in a deep saucepan. I serve it with melted butter to which I've added a squeeze of lemon juice, and Ralph cuts wafer-thin bread and butter from Verena's home-made bread.

One fights dandelions so in the garden, I try to remember to pick their leaves to mix into salads. Once, driving up France on a spring Sunday, we were puzzled to see field after field dotted with people walking slowly with bowed heads. We stopped so that we could see into their baskets, and realized they were picking young dandelion leaves.

Reg's planting list is still quite long in May:

> Chicory (Witloof)
> Chicory (Sugar loaf)
> Salsify
> Sow lettuce, radish, carrot,
>     spring onion every 10–14 days
> Runner beans

Peas (Oregon)
Sweetcorn

The boxes of annuals are ready to go out, when the plants they replace are finally over . . . stocks, petunias, tobacco plant, asters, antirrhinums.

This garden grows too much! I wake up almost hysterical under a load of ground elder, and rose leaves curling from some quite invisible insect, and think 'What can I do? What can I do? I shall never catch up, it's all racing past me.' But then comes the forgiving evening. Cooking dinner, I go into the garden to pick some herbs, and the cool envelopes me like water. Ralph says he's going to serve a drink in the summerhouse, but it won't be perfect there for much longer, so I'd better hurry . . . I fling on some other clothes (as when at sea on *Mary Deare*, I could never enjoy a pre-dinner drink in my day's dirt and cooking heat). Then I walk down the drive to the summerhouse and see that astonishing mountain of flowers at the gate, theatrical in the evening light. The white lilac seems luminous. There's a little miniature lilac bush beside the drive, a mound of paler mauve. The big lilacs are too far away for their scent to reach me, it's the honeysuckle on the side of the summerhouse I smell now.

The summer can be paced by the angle at which the sun shines into the summerhouse at this time. By the end of May it is far round to the right, over the stream. There is no wind, birds are the only movement. Swallows ceaselessly darting; blackbirds standing on their favourite look-outs. A thrush on the roof of the house pouring out song and the broken coos of those exotic doves that moved over England from Eastern Europe a few years ago.

Later, a misty moon in a sky empty of stars, and the lit jets scorching over between us and the moon, but the birds never stop twittering and chirping and singing. Later still, I saw the moon had come sharply clear, with one brilliant attendant star in a soft sky – but the lawns looked luminous, like pools, with white mist, and swathes of mist lay like bars across the trees.

# JUNE

# JUNE

'Only the soft unseeing Heaven of June,
The ghosts of great trees, and the sleeping flowers.'

FRANCIS BRETT YOUNG

I think 'softness' is the special quality of June. Often cool and moist after the heatwave that comes in May, there are evenings in June only made perfect by a light fire of ash logs. Sitting by it you can look out to the garden dripping with roses, and at the bowls of sweet peas in the room! I'm always surprised by the first roses and the first sweet peas, lovely of course, but also it's frightening that the year has come so far; how has half of it rushed past me? The spring gone already and the long pale evenings of midsummer here. Can nothing slow it down? Every summer I remember our first gardener Snow White telling us about the garden when we arrived saying, 'You've got the prettiest roses here I ever did see! Like great baskets of flowers they are!' He was speaking of the climbers and ramblers trained very high in two lines across the garden. Now I have pale ones behind the white border; two New Dawn, Alfred Carrière, Smith's White Climber, Frau Karl Drushki; the heavenly old Alberic Barbier who stretches her arms so wide they thread through her neighbours on either side. We replaced the wooden pillars when they rotted, with square pillars of dark red brick, the top cross-piece of wood. Summers when the roses are all in good heart – no deaths, or replacements still small – the line of flowering branches is continuous from end to end of the seven pillars. The other climbers are beyond the house, bordering the further lawn. Here we have cages of four thin wooden poles, and when I've managed to twine the roses round each pole and they pour over the top, they are indeed pillars of roses. Again New Dawn (here before we were), an equally old Emily Gray lost to a bad winter, is now replaced by

83

Coronna, and her contemporary Paul Scarlet by Altissimo. An exuberant Crimson Shower died off then grew four new roots, one at each corner of her cage, and is now better than ever. An American pillar (not my favourite rose), but I would not disturb her as she, too, was here before we were – and indeed she is a pretty sight at the end of the drive when her red and white flowers cover the whole of her support. Opposite her on the other side of the entrance to the lawn, is a climbing Speks yellow, impossibly difficult to keep down to its support, it will shoot upwards, but the pointed yellow roses are lovely. At the end of this line we had a scented musk – very early, cream turning to white, big sprays of small blossoms. I was appalled when this sickened and died (frost following drought, I think, and, being at the top of a bank, too sharp drainage). I cannot find this one on the market or learn its name, though a friend has several in her old garden. Reg managed to raise cuttings from my last pruning and so now she is replaced back in her old corner doing well and wonderfully fragrant. Because she is so early I have planted a red summer clematis Ernest Markham with her. Counting the cutting as legitimate descent, that makes five roses pouring out bloom which were planted in the 1920s when our predecessor laid out the garden after the restoration of the house shortly following the First World War. Sixty years! They are all long-known roses, expected to last. How right Vita Sackville-West was when she said 'but what is an old rose?' She was speaking of the white rose at Knole planted in the time of Charles II.

Sweet peas we grow in a little row in the kitchen garden in the old-fashioned way on pea sticks, because they look so much prettier than regimented on wires or poles; Reg saves our own seed, and gets more with five blooms than four, and many with six – very frilly. We sow half a row in autumn and half in spring, to spread the season.

My most vivid impression of June came to me by chance, early one morning, picking the sweet peas. For some reason I woke much earlier than usual and went into the garden. Yiwara as usual wandered round smelling for information about whoever had visited her territory during the night. I saw a mass of flowers above the kitchen garden and went to pick them. We'd had a week of high winds and grey skies, but this morning magic had come suddenly. There was no sound, no movement. I felt no one else in the world was astir, it belonged to me. There was an indescribable tenderness of light and colour, an intimacy, a freshness. The softest possible blue suffused the sky. Every leaf and petal was shining and extended, individually alive. The colours of all the flowers seemed luminous, just put on. You moved from scent to scent. The dew on the grass began to glimmer as the light grew. It was exciting, like an unexpected promise – and as fleeting.

Half an hour later it was just a lovely summer day. People were about, cars went through the village, the birds were moving all over the garden, breakfasting. It was as if a tryst had ended – a secret world glimpsed then vanished.

One of the joys of June is the rock roses, in clumps on the terrace as well as in the rockeries. Sitting in the dining-room window seat they all turn their faces to the house (to the sun). Clumps of yellow and red and pink and bronze and white. The flowers only last a day, gone by lunch time, new ones tomorrow. The rock plants are Ralph's special thing because he built the rockeries while waiting for the result of a big film sale that was pending. Impossible to concentrate on work in such suspense! So he sleuthed out a local sand pit where they'd disinterred and discarded a lot of magnificent Ice Age glacier stones. When the truck delivered them I thought it would break up the paving of the drive, it was so heavy. He manhandled them into position with an iron bar along the slope where there had been rockeries before, but less ambitious ones.

His were miniature mappin terraces (now so clothed in flowers he has work to clear the handsome framework). With his usual thoroughness, he bought different categories of rock plants, some for sharp drainage, some for deep pockets of soil between rocks, some for a moraine. There are little paths, natural steps, a deep unexpected pool half hidden. From earliest spring to midsummer, this area below the drive is alight with wave after wave of flowers. After the rock roses come the rock pinks in great profusion. All these pinks, infinitely varied in colour, size and pattern, are from a packet of seed I bought for Ralph's 'new rockery' when visiting his parents in Sussex. They took me into Brighton to see a Regency exhibition at the Pavilion, where (I cannot think why) they sold flower seeds. Ralph was in Arabia at the time, gathering the impressions that resulted in *The Doomed Oasis*. He sowed them all when he came home.

The garden has six stone seats strategically placed. A spring one under the lilac tree, in a corner of the first lawn. One beside the pools, one hidden in a lonicera hedge beside the white border. One facing towards the further garden from the end of the white border; one at the end of the rose garden. The one I use most is beside the front door. I covered two long cushions in dark blue plastic, one for this, the other to take where you like. In summer I have my morning tea on the seat beside the door. Later the coffee, which is my breakfast, and afternoon tea when it's too hot in the summerhouse.

In the four beds of hybrid teas running down from the house – so you see them massed – I have mixed colours intentionally, mixed heights unintentionally, though I rather like the irregularity. I am greatly comforted in my gardening mistakes and failures by the comment a friend of mine made about someone we both knew: 'Oh, my dear, it's a stockbroker's garden. Every rose bush measured for size, and weed just a four-letter word.'

Now my white border comes to life. The Solomon's Seal is first, then clumps of white irises, and next the huge white poppies with their purple-black centres and wonderfully crumpled petals; white pinks, the old Mrs Sinkins, so profuse, but quickly over; Madonna lilies with their heady scent; a tall feathery spiraea (aruncus), and a low spiraea which is the garden version of meadowsweet, creamy flowers on red stalks and fern-like leaves (filipendula fl.pl.), astilbe, campanulas. The tall white delphiniums are beginning; they are the queens of this border, groups of tremendous spikes visible from all over the garden, framed between the red brick pillars of roses.

The herbaceous border beside the drive has to be cleared of the crocus foliage along the front and the daffodil leaves at the back, a dreary job. One can't live without bulbs – the burgeoning life of each new year – but their dead leaves make the garden look ragged. Apart from pansies, which seem impervious to season, the little red geum Miss Wilmott is the first flower; the lovely red foliage of the astilbe clumps decorate the border long before the flowers, and the pyracanthas on the wall of the house mass their white flowers. I'm gradually catching up on my early summer border, which I'd never bothered about – never saw – during the years we were sailing. My only coloured irises were some given me by a neighbour when we first came, and she apologized then for their being old! I don't think they like this border, they flower much better on the bank above the herb bed. I bought a packet of lupin seed at our church flower festival, and these flower splendidly, but unfortunately you can't tell the colours till too late! I put a few clumps of annuals into this border, tobacco plants and stocks; they continue flowering so late and seem to carry summer on into autumn – unlike chrysanthemums, which seem to carry winter into any season.

Every year it's a problem when to scrap the wallflowers from the tubs, losing the last of their scent and colour; we replace them on each side of the summerhouse with fuschias and begonias, and by the front door with geraniums; I mix the colours as much as possible, the clashes are so exciting. The planting list has dwindled to the sowing every ten days or so of lettuce, radish, carrot, spring onion, mustard-and-cress, which continues throughout the summer. Now we are eating the results!

New peas, asparagus, young carrots; the trouble is they all need butter, and one must limit this unless one is to risk ballooning utterly. I resist (except occasionally for best) cooking peas in the perfect way; melt 'enough' butter in a thick saucepan, put in some lettuce, preferably hearts, with a few tiny onions and the peas, shake them together and put a lid on; when the butter is absorbed sprinkle with salt and sugar and add just enough boiling water to cover, simmer till tender. This should be served as a dish on its own, I think.

If there isn't enough asparagus for a dish by itself, the tips, lightly cooked, make a lovely filling for an omelette.

The first globe artichokes are ready – more butter! I remember seeing the streets of Roscoff, the little Normandy town which supplies them to Paris, and many other parts of France, piled high with great mountains of globe artichokes to stop the traffic! This was in protest at the low price the government had set for them. I

was amazed at the variety in the market; the flat-based prickly ones, the smooth egg-shaped kind; purple varieties, white varieties. The people there think cooking spoils them, and prefer eating them raw, a taste I cannot share; hot with butter or cold with vinaigrette, I like them cooked. Whenever I cut them, I remember those big muscular women in the market at Roscoff wrenching off the thick hairy stalks by hand. When one of our artichoke plants sets more than it can possibly develop, I try to catch some young enough – the size of a pullet's egg or less – to put in boiling water for a few minutes, or if really tiny, just marinate in oil and lemon, and serve cold as an hors d'oeuvre as I have so often eaten them in France. They need daily watching, or else one day you see from afar those brilliant blue flowers – you have lost them then.

These evenings the setting sun slants in through the north window of the kitchen, making red and gold patterns on the dark beams and the white wall, and I have a jug of herb-flowers on the table; blue borage and mauve applemint, white fennel (the small kind grown for its seeds), marjoram, rosemary, lavender. They're said to keep flies away. We are not troubled by flies, but they smell so nice!

At last the day's work is over and the time comes to sleep. It is difficult to go indoors from the soft moist lovely night of scents and dew and stillness, everything standing as if painted, the willows very fluffy. The long white nights of June when you barely lose the colour of the roses before the light comes again. Just a few dark hours to sleep away before another lovely day begins.

# JULY

# JULY

'Can you tell me where has hid her
Pretty maid July?
I would swear that I do know
The blue bliss of her eye.'

FRANCIS THOMPSON

July is the month when you can luxuriate in the sense of summer – the open doors, the warmth, the flowers, the long evenings – feeling that this way of life will last for ever; last winter has sunk below the horizon, next winter not yet cast its shadow. It's a dainty lighthearted month. My long blue cushion stays overnight on the seat beside the door. The garden flutters with birds catching their breakfast. The night-scented stock is still luminous – every year Reg sows little patches of it at intervals along the border. The garden is fresh with dew but the sun is already warm.

Of course it isn't always like this. But a cold grey day in July is an affront – just a mistake. 'Where has hid her pretty maid July?'

There is so much to pick I have to take the biggest trug round the garden. It is at this season of full growth that Reg's good neighbourly relationship with weeds is most trying. One needs protective clothing to approach the kitchen garden – gumboots, long gloves, sometimes a leather jacket, to fight one's way between the rows. But the crops are wonderful. In the fruit cage, tearing off the veil of bindweed from each clump, there are colanders full of delicious strawberries. There is a special summery feeling about picking strawberries, because a strawberry bed is always put in the warmest place. Those that ripen in our absence, Verena preserves in her delectable jam that tastes like fresh fruit.

The next peas to 'turn in' are the Petits Pois – tight little pods absolutely full, growing in pairs, very profuse. Slow work to fill a basin with them, they are so small and the pods so tight. The broad beans are still young and tender and all green, not having made their grey jackets yet. I serve them with Elizabeth David's egg and lemon sauce; the yolks of two eggs, the juice of a lemon whipped up over slow heat with a cup of the water the beans were boiled in, until it is frothy and thickened slightly.

Sometimes a mistake turns out well enough to repeat it. I tried to make a mayonnaise in too much hurry – was out of practice – it wouldn't 'make'. It was a thick yellow sauce, but not a mayonnaise. (I must have let too much oil slip in.) So I abandoned it. The next day I found I'd used up all the eggs with the wretched thing and had none left to make the egg and lemon sauce for the beans. So I whipped up the failed mayonnaise and added the cup of hot bean stock to that, and left it in the lower oven of the Aga for a little while. It really was delicious. Ralph said 'a cross between hot mayonnaise and lemon meringue pie without the meringue'. I must do it again.

The courgettes are ready almost before one needs them. The confusion in the seed catalogues between courgette and zucchini seems absolute. To me they are classified as I found, bought and cooked them during the years when we sailed from one end of the Mediterranean to the other. 'Courgette' are the thin dark green cucumber-like ones of France; 'zucchini' take over when you leave the French coast and sail east to Italian, Greek and Turkish shores. They are shorter, fatter, more egg-shaped, lighter in colour and faintly striped green and yellow. The flavour is not quite as good as the true courgette. I first remember these at a luncheon at Government House in Malta (when the Dormans were there). A vast dish came round filled with neat rows and rows of them, well matched for size; little golden green bundles, tender and buttery, it was one of the prettiest dishes I have ever seen and set me a standard, trying to emulate it on a small scale. For the true courgette I frequently use Elizabeth David's method of cooking them in butter with a ghost of garlic, then adding strips of lean ham. I cut them in rounds, not too thin, I never dice – if big enough to dice they are past their best. I always remember the downgrading of courgettes in the Mediterranenan greengrocers – even the little back street shops of small ports. At the front of the shop today's picking, each courgette wearing its fresh yellow flower. Halfway back are yesterday's, with the flowers wilting. And at the back of the shop, relegated so shamefully, poor things, those that are two days old, with the flowers hanging down shrivelled.

The battle with courgettes is to keep them picked before they get too large and the plants cease producing new ones. (Some that really get away from us we leave for winter soups, but we grow another kind of large and round gourd which is really better for this.) Courgette make a lovely and quite substantial salad. They are good raw, but I prefer them put in boiling water for not more than five minutes, so they don't lose their firmness. When cold I slice them into rounds, dress them with a lot of marjoram, olive oil and lemon, black pepper and coarse salt.

The cucumbers start in July in the greenhouse, and are very prolific. I go into a routine of making cucumber sandwiches for tea, as Ralph is inordinately fond of them. We have discovered a new variety of tomatoes which also turn in by mid-July. We grow them in a frame. They are small, when mature scarcely the size of a ping-pong ball; bright red, a good flavour, very pretty, we have never had tomatoes so early before. Cos lettuces I think it a pity to slice, those lovely central leaves are so crisp! I stack them standing-up in a deep dish and we dip them into a little bowl of garlicky mayonnaise. The new season's carrots are still small enough to eat raw with thick cream or yoghurt. Generally there are radishes. The dwarf French beans are always ready before one expects them, easy to pick in bunches, finger-length, to cook lightly in boiling water and eat whole, of course, with melted butter, marjoram or chives and a squeeze of lemon juice.

Mangetout, the peas eaten whole while they are still flat, are another crop one has to watch daily, as they hide in their leaves and are difficult to see, and there are always more than you think! We tried to grow these in early days, but I didn't realize you had to pick them before the peas begin to swell, and we had no joy of them. Oddly enough, I discovered how exquisite they are at 10 Downing Street, when Edward Heath invited us to the dinner he gave in honour of Gough Whitlam, then Prime Minister of Australia. Ralph had just published his Australian novel, *Golden Soak* – or perhaps Mr Heath just wanted to have some sailing people there. It was quite a moment of history, I think, a socialist Prime Minister of Australia proposing the toast to the Queen in 10 Downing Street. He did it perfectly, then made an impeccable speech. The very fine string quartet which had played during dinner plunged (there is no other word) into Waltzing Matilda. 'They've never heard it played like that before!' one of my partners whispered. But the association of sugar peas, mangetout, with that evening is indelible. Having seen what they should be like, we have grown them since with great success. They had then accompanied an excellent duck dish, by the way. (Throw the mangetout into boiling salty water, but take out while still crisp.)

It always seems tantalizing that raspberries overlap strawberries. If only there were a gap between, to spread the largesse! I know lemon juice, or better still fresh lime juice, is supposed to be the perfect thing with them, but I still like cream and sugar. With wood strawberries the juice is better – you don't taste it, it just brings out the flavour of the fruit. We have a little row of wood strawberries, never very many, but from early to late summer always some to sprinkle over anything else. Red currants I like because they're so pretty; white currants are the only ones I really enjoy eating and we've lost ours in the bad winter. Black currants Verena makes into purée which is bottled for future sorbets (or colds in the head).

I like to give a party in mid-July, partly for the roses, but chiefly for Ralph's birthday on the 15th, St Swithin's Day. Some years the lines of tall climbers really are at their best, pillars of roses, the bush roses full of flowers, and the white delphiniums and lilies still beautiful. This is one of the things I think more important to the host and hostess than to the guests, who after all have their own roses, and are probably too busy talking to notice. Our tall willows to the west block the sun by party time anyhow, so the centre of the garden is shadowy, and becomes vivid again at the end.

I fill the pitcher on the stairs with long sprays of roses and syringa flowing through the banisters, and a big silver punch bowl at the foot of the stairs with anything pale – roses, Madonna lilies, late peonies. Then the brightest red roses I have, packed into the old coptic bowl on the mantelpiece at the other end of the hall, under the silvery-grey John Newton picture.

Verena makes her crisp and dainty cheese straws; sometimes we have sausages with a mustard dip, always angels-on-horseback (tinned smoked oysters rolled in very thin bacon, served crispy hot in my mother's silver entrée dishes); cold we have diced cheddar cheese and crystallized ginger together on sticks, apricots stuffed with mozzarella cheese and chopped walnuts; nuts and crisps; sometimes a dip, perhaps cottage cheese with chopped shrimps.

One summer of great heat I was having a pre-prandial drink on the seat beside the front door when the first guests arrived. I went down the drive to meet them, then others came, then a steady stream, and so perfect was the evening, we never managed to get the party indoors! – it just went on in the drive and on the terrace. Verena and Nora brought the drinks out, then the food, realizing the people were immovable. So no one saw my flowers in the house! – but it's no good regimenting people when they're happy. If I'd known, I'd have laid everything out in the summerhouse and everyone could have spread about from there, but I never do plan a party out of doors; too fearful a nature, I suppose, or perhaps I've suffered too many that were cold (Istanbul) or insect-ridden (Peru).

It is the nights of summer that give life a different dimension. Instead of being sharply divided into indoors, outdoors, darkness and light, time blurs and softens to the changing lights and airs and movements of the garden.

One day during the summer when my second book, *What Lands Are These?*, was published, I had been in London in blazing heat and given three interviews and a photo session in one day. Ralph drove me home straight from Broadcasting House after I had recorded the last interview. We arrived in time to hear it and it seemed to go well. I was on a wave of euphoria, too excited to sleep, so I went into the garden. There was an almost full moon, but it was still below the house, I couldn't see it from the drive so I went down the steps past the summerhouse. A whiff of jasmine mixed with the scent of the night scented stock. From the walk beside the stream I could see the moon, bright and clear above the roof. I sat on one of the square stone tops that we have on either side of a little flight of steps. These tops are Farthing Stones, so called because in the past children were paid a farthing for each

stone in which they pricked holes all over, while it was still hot, for use in the bakeries. We have them in the paths too, making a pattern with flints and bricks.

The cool calm was like a benison. It was so quiet that a frog splashing into the pool was startling. A soft little owl call came from somewhere along the willows, always so fluffy and thick at night, and another owl answered it from further away. Yiwara had come out with me and I saw her long black back slipping through the bushes, looking for hedgehogs. But how a garden belongs to itself at night, shaking off human domination! One's own familiar, worked-over garden becomes a strange wild place, in which one walks as a stranger, almost an intruder.

I have sometimes thought that on summer nights Miss Cook is down by the lily ponds. She was the unmarried sister of a previous owner, and I think this garden was her creative thing in life and that she cared for it deeply. Only twice in all the years have I felt she was there, but it was a very strong presence. I imagined her calm and smiling, sitting quietly on the stone seat beside the pools enjoying the garden she had made. I've always thought she was the haunt in the corner of the east bedroom – a small spare room not often slept in, but which I use as a work room for machining, et cetera. For years I would not enter that room alone at night.

It's strange how localized such presences are – not only one room, but one part of the room has the invisible barrier of fear. I've known this in two other houses, and you always know exactly where it is. Nora once went to speak to Verena who was cleaning this room and found the presence so strong she couldn't enter but had to talk to Verena from the landing. She only mentioned it years later, not knowing whether I had noticed anything, and seeing no point in suggesting it. I had indeed noticed it, though not as strongly as she had (in daylight with someone working in the room!). She is a Highlander, I am a Borderer, and Verena is Suffolk. But Verena, when very young, had known Miss Cook, and known this room when it was her bedroom, which would make a difference.

This feeling has faded gradually and I can now go in at night – perhaps she has come to accept me because I too love and serve the garden. The dangerous place is a large built-in wardrobe in the far corner. It used to have a beautiful narrow oak door, but we took this down to the study for the entrance to the passage, and replaced it with curtains. Sometimes I still cannot go there at night without putting on the lights, propping the door open, singing and hurrying out again, with a frisson at the back of my neck. But I think she is mellowing.

The garden was now very black and white with moonlight, and quite still. Even the owls had stopped. I called Yiwara but she didn't come. I found her nuzzling a hedgehog on the lawn. It didn't seem alarmed, it didn't even bother to put its prickles up, but I collected her and we went in, while the hedgehog made off into the bushes with that surprising turn of speed they sometimes show.

# AUGUST

# AUGUST

'Go not, happy day
From the shining fields.'

TENNYSON

August is the month when Provence steps into the garden. 'But not those bloody red and green tomatoes,' Ralph says. They had been on my every shopping list in the Eastern Mediterranean; as they were one of the few things I could always get, I relied on them for salads and sauces. I don't think these coarse red and green field tomatoes, 'vegetable tomatoes', compare for flavour with the round red English tomatoes – or 'Channel Island' tomatoes as a French greengrocer at Loch Tudi called them when she showed them to me with excited pride one year: 'Now we can get these! They are delicious, like a fruit!'

Our peppers (capsicum) had started in July, now the aubergines are catching up. Reg has lifted the onions and shallots, so juicy and sweet when new. The big greenhouse tomatoes are turning from scarlet to crimson, and the miniature tomatoes, which have been such a joy, are now red on the outdoor bushes. I look up all the recipes for stuffing peppers and aubergines, revive my memory of Iman Bayeldi, of melanzane salad, of piperade, of ratatouille, which I love so much I will even make it for myself sometimes if alone. There are still some French beans small enough to eat. Again my thoughts turn to the French greengrocers, and how tiny, threadlike, they sell *haricots verts* (the slightly larger ones are cheaper, as being inferior).

The custard marrows (later than courgettes) are ready, such decorative little patty-pan objects. A friend of mine inspects hers every morning, and picks them as soon as the flowers drop. I am not so methodical, but they should never be larger than the top of a teacup. I arrange these little fluted ivory things in a fireproof dish, sprinkle with olive oil, salt and pepper, cover with tinfoil and bake till just tender. They take a little longer than courgettes, and I think it is better to chop the herbs over them when they are cooked. They have less flavour than courgettes so take stronger herbs, mint or tarragon or even fennel. If you want to make it a main dish for a hot night, you can sprinkle it with grated cheese, or chopped hard-boiled egg, or coarsely choppped nuts, or pine kernels, or prawns. They make a nice salad, too, raw. I slice them thinly downwards to show the fluted shape, dress them with vinaigrette first and then a little mayonnaise or yoghurt, sprinkle with chopped shallot and mint, or a lot of lemon balm.

Now there are so many cucumbers I make iced soup. I think this is nicest with raw cucumbers, their flavour doesn't seem to survive cooking. I peel them and if they are outdoor ones with a core of seeds, I take this out whole with a potato peeler, then chop roughly and emulsify with a light stock – chicken, or the strained stock of white fish, or – much better! – salmon stock. When smooth, sieve for perfection, add cream or quite a lot of top of milk, sprinkle with chopped mint, or chives, or both, and chill. A Norwegian friend, chatting in her kitchen, opened my eyes to the use of fish stocks. 'We value it and use it just as much as you use meat or poultry stock!' she said. 'Everyone learns to make the best use of what they have most of!'

With fish I serve cucumber salad the way I always ate it in Norway, with a sweet oily dressing in which you hardly notice any vinegar or lemon (the lemon is on the fish). With anything else I grate a little mint over the cucumber, and use a straight vinaigrette.

When I am really overwhelmed by cucumbers, I do, rather against my principles, use one as a vegetable. Cut it into chunks – I don't peel unless it's a rough-skinned one – and steam till just tender. Meanwhile, bring to the boil a cup of double cream with a dash of lemon juice and a little salt, simmer and stir till as thick as you wish, add a chopped herb, marjoram or basil or parsley, and pour over the cucumber pieces, which it is essential to drain very well before arranging them in the serving dish. Whatever you do they will make more moisture, so it is wise to keep cucumber and cream hot separately, and only combine when ready to serve.

A salad satisfying enough to make a hot evening's supper dish is this bean and courgette and egg dish. Most young vegetables are good cold with a vinaigrette, but small French beans are best of all. We grow both green and yellow ones, and they look pretty mixed. Picked finger-length, thrown briefly into salted boiling water, taken out whole they still snap, and dressed while hot with olive oil, black pepper and salt – a squeeze of lemon juice later. Pile them in the centre of a dish when cold, on top of them arrange very small courgettes, lightly steamed or baked, anoint with the same dressing, and sprinkle thickly with pine kernels or sliced almonds. Surround this pile with halved hard-boiled eggs, coated with sour cream and sprinkled with paprika.

The first cabbages can be made summery, too, as a very dainty coleslaw. Shred the tender green leaves finely, and combine with the first peppers, too small to stuff, cut into thin strips after removing pith and seeds. If the crop is heavy, they need picking so those left can mature. Add a sprinkling of green onions. Quite a strong herb, even thyme, goes well.

This will take a more elaborate dressing. For instance, to your usual French dressing, add finely chopped watercress, parsley, tarragon, capers, dill cucumbers, hard-boiled egg, a grating of horseradish, and perhaps a little tomato purée. Stir well together, but only combine with the coleslaw just before serving.

When it's too hot to be in the garden in the afternoon, I sometimes come into the cool kitchen and prepare a dish for supper, so there's nothing to do when the lovely evening comes. Salmon is not the only fish good cold – but the others depend more on herbs and salads. I like poached fillets of sole, which provide two dishes.

Allow at least two for each person. Buy the bones and head, and simmer with onion and carrot and bay leaf. It's worth bothering to shell a few prawns or shrimps for the wonderful addition their shells make to the stock. Leave to simmer for at least an hour. Strain, add a dash of white wine, and in this liquor poach the fillets, folded into neat little bundles. They cook very quickly, don't let them risk breaking. Lift them out and leave to drain. Meanwhile strain the liquor again, add a dash of Pernod, taste for salt and pepper, and pour into the bowls you mean to serve it in. It will set to a beautiful fine jelly. When cold, put in fridge for garden lunch tomorrow. Before serving, sprinkle with chopped tarragon, and serve with lemon quarters and thin brown bread and butter sprinkled with chopped walnuts or hazelnuts.

When the sole fillets are cold, arrange on a shallow dish and coat with mayonnaise or sour cream in which you have chopped anchovy fillets, tarragon and chives. Surround with any greenery you have, decorate with the prawns or shrimps, and serve with a green salad and potato salad; the potatoes are young enough to slice, not dice, and sliced young carrots mix well with them.

And with fish . . . Muscadet! We have a great affection for this wine, which we discovered at the beginning of our sailing life, round the coasts of Normandy and Brittany. You couldn't find it anywhere else in those days, but in the little fish restaurants, which were a wonderful reward at the end of those rocky estuaries, they brought it automatically. So many nights I sat in some dimly-lit little bare dining-room, eating bread and perhaps soup or an omelette or some shrimps to occupy myself and pass the time, while Ralph and the friends sailing with us guzzled plates of mussels – which I can't eat because they make my face swell, and I don't like them anyway. Somehow I remember the Muscadet in such places even better than in the lovely restaurants – as at Lézardrieux, where we watched Sophie Brenner and her husband, who was a great chef by any standards, rise from the little Hôtel du Commerce down by the quay, to the great hotel they built, with lights shining down the estuary.

The last time we dined there, wonderfully welcomed as old friends, we saw a whole line of yellow oilskins hung up by diners; and as there was only one other yacht in the harbour that night, we asked about them. Sophie giggled and whispered, 'No, they are not sailing! They have driven, some from as far as Paris, but they have heard it is a yachting pub, so they think it is *très chic* to come in oilskins!' And at a superb restaurant at the Baie des Anges at l'Aberwrac'h, Madame had the finest Muscadet we've ever tasted. She told us the name of the very small vineyard it came from, and I asked for it everywhere we dined down the Biscay coast, but no one had even heard of it; until, at Île d'Yeu, in an excellent restaurant whose owner had been chef to a king, he said, 'Yes, yes I know it! It is wonderful, but alas I have none, it is very difficult to get, and I have not enough people here who would appreciate it. Where did you have it? Ah, yes! Madame at the Baie des Anges . . . She is lucky.'

Then one day in London, walking down St James's Street, I saw the whole window of a wine shop displaying Muscadet, and I thought, 'Ah! My little sailing wine is getting around.' Gradually it appeared on every wine list. Last year we visited one of the vineyards in the huge area now producing it, near the mouth of the Loire, and the son of the owner confirmed my early memories. 'In those days Muscadet was not sent even to Paris, it was just a local wine. Now . . . ! I will show you our export list. It came up very quickly.' Someone who helped bring this about is our old friend Gabor Denes, who first came into our lives as a sailing photographer taking pictures of ourselves and our boat for Ralph's publisher, and proved a charming and most seamanlike guest on board our first ocean-racer, *Triune of Troy*. Then he settled for the gourmet side of his interests and wrote a wine and food column. He, too, had fallen in love with Muscadet when sailing round northern France, and promoted it. Now whenever we meet him we drink a bottle in happy memory.

August has been everybody's holiday month since schooldays, a fat, blowsy, lazy month. Even if you're working hard, there's a relaxed feeling because so many other people are on holiday. You have time to 'stand and stare'.

The summer Yiwara was a puppy, we had a rabbit in the garden. When we are between dogs, the wild breaks in, which explains why our dogs, when adult, are so assiduous at beating the bounds and keeping an eye on everything. It was a very young rabbit, and took up residence at the end of the garden near the watersplash; indeed, it used to go right up to our fence where there was a gap in the hedge to watch the people, and sit there washing his face, so he became quite well known. As Yiwara hadn't yet ventured so far afield, they hadn't discovered each other. One evening we and two friends who were dining with us had been watching Yiwara through the window. Like all sheepdog puppies she devised elaborate games for herself, but hers were more am- bitious and varied than the play of any dog I've ever watched. It was fascinating to see the planned routines of crouch, dart, creep, circle; the varied timing, the area she covered. When we went outside, of course, she stopped, looked self-conscious, wandered off, then started playing again, but less ambitiously. Suddenly we noticed the rabbit was also playing by himself, on top of the little box hedge surrounding one of the sundial beds. He too devised routines, running, stopping to sit up and look around, hopping, sometimes staging a fast run round the entire hedge. Down at their level they were screened by bushes, so the two young animals continued to play in their separate playgrounds, each unaware of the other.

At this time of year, when I go across the bridge in the evening to pick fruit for dinner, I will see a duck has settled her family into the bank of the stream for the night – all those tiny fluffy balls nestled into the grass! She may make mild cautionary noises, but she doesn't really mind me. During the daytime, a Muscovy regularly brings her brood on quite a long expedition, up from the stream, round outside our garden, and along the path on the far side, for them to eat some special plant she cannot find elsewhere. She regiments them neatly, and they keep together well as they follow her, but it seems a dangerous journey.

All my life a chill finger has been laid on this month, as first my mother and now my husband can be relied on to say, on some radiant August morning when a perfect summer day is obviously beginning, 'There's a touch of autumn in the air this morning!' This enrages me, I who will always turn my back to any approaching tide. And yet, and yet . . . the apples have turned colour enough to show on the trees. And the swallows are gathering on the telephone wires. They begin to collect long before they finally take off on their unimaginable journey, and the numbers grow slowly, but one senses their preparation. They are always flying about the garden, swirling and criss-crossing; feeding, yes; but perhaps exercising their wings for the long flight over land and sea; getting to know each other? Choosing leaders? The martins mingle with them, but the swifts keep separate, always seven of them – parents with five young? – they swoop and dive and scream in tight formation, carefree, playing. The willow seeds drift across the garden, fairy wisps of fluff, the air is never empty in August. The colours of the border are deeper, rich reds and purples and golds, red and

pink and blue phlox, blue salvias, clumps of hellenium brown and yellow. I have a golden-rod described as dwarf, certainly it is not leggy like the old-fashioned kind. About three feet tall, it makes wonderfully dense soft clumps of gold. Edging the drive now are little clumps of pansies and carnations in front, and one or two fill-in clumps of stocks. A few tall dahlias give brilliant emphasis.

The white border begins to thin when the white phlox and marguerites fade. Now there will only be a few white dahlias, shasta daisies and the tall perennial chrysanthemums, fluffy and lovely, but short-lived, and later white michaelmas daisies and a few white chrysanthemums. I must introduce some silver leaf plants, yuccas perhaps, and prolong the life of the white border. The lovely tobacco plants stay with us so long, red and pink and green and white. The herb border is in flower, the bright borage which sows itself everywhere, the flat great yellow heads of the fennel, marjoram's dainty mauve flowers. The bright mauve cushions of the chives are over.

The roses are patchy, but heavy with buds for a second crop. The Mermaid on the house, always a late rose and here facing north, is now lit with the wide open pale yellow single flowers. A strange thing happened; a photograph appeared in a newspaper of Ralph sitting on the seat beside the front door, with an Alsatian beside him. Verena's sharp eyes noticed the Mermaid was very small, only just beginning; it must be a very old photograph they'd dug out. So which dog was it? We looked more closely and recognized Blair, come back from the shades to be seen again sitting beside his master, the dog of the house.

The full greenery everywhere is soporific. A leisure, a lingering is upon us. 'The evenings are drawing in,' someone is sure to say, and I cannot deny it. Now the sun shines straight into the summer-house at teatime, almost reaching the vivid blue tiles of the two Ajulajos panels which a previous owner, who loved Portugal, had had built into the back wall, one of St Christopher with the Child in his arms, the other of a castle. A white clematis on the outside of this wall always comes through at the top and falls down inside in a slender cascade of translucent white blossoms and leaves.

Now, every morning when I wake, I look first out of the window to count (unless there are too many) the radiant blue flowers of the morning glory which have come out in the night, new every day, a visitation, we train a few plants up the rose posts. This corner of the lawn is where Francis Chichester, when he and Sheila stayed with us, repaired to do his yoga exercises at the beginning of the day. Yla (Yiwara's aunt), who followed him, observed with interest the spectacle, new to her, of a man standing on his head. She decided he might be vulnerable to his enemies in such a defence-less position, so sat down in a place carefully chosen to guard him from any approach. This conscientious protection slightly bothered Francis when he was ready to come in for breakfast. 'I thought she might fancy a tasty morsel of me,' he said. Sheila had no such qualms – her unshakeable calm would give confidence to any animal.

The full moon comes at the end of August – the harvest moon. They say she stays at the full two nights running, to help with the harvest. Huge and yellow, lovely but almost unnatural, like a great lantern in the sky, shining for a very long time with an air of leisure as if aware she had two nights to be seen at her best; shining so tranquilly over the tawny fields and dark greenery – full and calm, the very epitome of August. But today I saw the first red leaves on the cherry tree.

# SEPTEMBER

# SEPTEMBER

'. . . to set budding more,
And still more, later flowers for the bees
Until they think warm days will never cease.'

KEATS

The summer goes on for ever. Only the sparkle is a warning, the garden seems lit by subtly hidden flood-lights – sometimes every leaf glitters.

It is heartbreaking to have to be away for September, as occasionally happens to us, and to leave the profuse bounty of the garden. There is so much – an explosion of crops everywhere, a wild rush of maturity, the seasons overlapping. The sweetcorn are perfect, golden and fully formed, but moist, not that darker colour which means hardness. There is an outburst of courgettes, so one can really pick them small enough, and tiny custard marrows. One almost forgets the climbing beans, they must wait, because there are some late globe artichokes. The aubergines are fully ripe, a good size and richly purple. The peppers are perfect now for stuffing, and one by one turn from green to scarlet to crimson. The cucumbers and tomatoes are ripe out of doors, and are almost as good in flavour as those from the greenhouse.

There's a heavy crop of Victoria plums this year, on one old tree, much better than on the new tree. The ground is covered with windfall apples. The roof of the greenhouse is hanging with bunches of grapes from the vine Reg trained there, casually, as an experiment, when it failed under cloches. Grapes make such beautifully-shaped bunches, no wonder they have been used as a design in so many different textures. (I have them in the Point de Venise lace tablecloth Ralph bought me in Cyprus, where the pattern survived in just one village, and was taken from there back to Venice, where it had been forgotten: and grapes combine with the Tudor rose

carved in the wooden bressummer above the drawing-room fire.)
There is a good crop of hazelnuts, the husks turning golden; they
are already full and sweet. The squirrels love them, there are piles
of empty shells under the tree. Yiwara likes them too, but prefers
walnuts. One of our rare good walnut years, when they were laid
out on trays in the boiler room (just to dry the outer shells, not,
of course, to risk their drying inside), their number was noticed to
diminish, and there were empty shells on the floor. Yiwara was
working through them.

When Reg mentions sprouts or cabbages I despair – they
belong to winter, I can't think about them now; now it must be all
the hot southern summer crops.

This is the richest colouring of the border's year. Clumps of
michaelmas daisies add blues and purples to contrast with the tall
pink and red windflowers, the soft gold blur of golden-rod, a few
late phlox, brown and yellow heleniums, the occasional bright
splashes of dahlias. Blue is good in the autumn border – the low
wiry plumbagoides is covered with bright blue flowers and its
leaves are turning scarlet. The roses are having an abundant second
crop, the tall white tobacco plants go luminous at night, gleaming
from far away. So do the evening primroses.

Coming in to the kitchen and setting down the loaded trug, it
seems too beautiful to dismantle. Once when I'd taken a basketful
like this to a London friend, she told me later that she'd left it in
her hall all day for people to admire – 'It was prettier than a bouquet.'

The late sun still shines in through the north window, touching
again the purple and scarlet and gold and green of the vegetables,
and illuminating a vase of herbs on the table; at this time the
garden seems to flow into the house.

What shall I do with all these things? The peppers, halved and
seeded, are nice stuffed with diced aubergine, a little green onion
and chopped mushroom, bound with beaten egg, pine kernels
sprinkled on top, anointed with olive oil and put in the oven. It's
quite a good idea to put a cupful of water in the pan, as when
roasting a bird. If you have tomatoes large enough, take their tops
off and seeds out and fill in the same way, and arrange in alternate
rows, serving in the ovenproof dish. Impossible to give a time, say
between half an hour and an hour in the top oven, but they will

transfer to a cool lower oven and wait happily if you are not ready. In Greece we were always seeing huge trays of these stuffed peppers and tomatoes carried above someone's head, being taken to the bakery for cooking, but the patron's wife at the restaurant on the quay at Pylos, whom I watched preparing them, cooked her own. She had no aubergine, but used just tomato and onion finely chopped, and uncooked rice; then a copious soaking in olive oil. I think aubergine is firm enough to take the place of the more usual rice or soaked breadcrumbs, and is a change when you happen to have them. Iman Bayeldi, that king of aubergine dishes, I make according to Elizabeth David's recipe.

I make a paté which follows the recipe for *tapénade* which the patron's wife of the auberge Mère Germaine at Chateau Neuf du Pape told me long ago, but sometimes using aubergine instead of tunny as the solid ingredient. I cook large ripe aubergines (bake in the oven, but they can be cooked in boiling water) till tender. Scoop out of the skin and mash with olive oil. Then ... '*les anchois, les olives noires, un gout de cognac, un tout petit peu de citron – et les tapénos, naturellement! les tapénos* (capers in Provençal).' She preferred a pestle and mortar to an electric blender, as the paté was rougher, had more character. I never use a blender for this, as unless you are making vast quantities you waste a lot. I chop the olives and the anchovy fillets as finely as I can, and the capers, mix into the mashed aubergine, add olive oil to make it all a stiff paste, add brandy and lemon to taste, pepper and salt as necessary. The proportions are a matter of taste. It's attractive smoothed into little pots, ramekins, one for each person, and served with thin toast or hot oatcakes as a first course. But don't bother unless you know your guests appreciate that sort of food. I made a superb *tapénade* once, and a guest said he thought it was sardine paste. . . .

I reluctantly do as the books say, and leave thickly-sliced aubergine sprinkled with salt in a colander for a while, 'to get rid of the bitter juices'. I'm not convinced our garden-raised ones have any bitter juices, but it does make them less hysterically absorbent, so you use less excessive quantities of oil. These thick slices, cut across, lengthways or obliquely, according to size, seem most at home fried in olive oil with chopped herbs (I like marjoram best, or basil) as an accompanying vegetable or by themselves. They are

good cold, dressed with yoghurt in which you have crushed a little garlic.

Peppers are nice raw, but need slicing thinly with kitchen scissors. Serbian salad, which I learned in Belgrade, was a great standby on *Mary Deare*, as salad ingredients were rare in the Eastern Mediterranean, and now we have it very often at home for lunch in the garden, to accompany cheeses and home-made bread. It consists of finely sliced tomatoes, finely sliced onions, and the thinly sliced peppers, with a French dressing.

The mushrooms and other edible fungus which suddenly arrive in the garden at this time of year are an act of God. Possibly they are descended from some bits and pieces we had thrown out after fungus-hunting expeditions, but they come up always in the same places; under the walnut tree, beside the summerhouse, and by the leaf-pile. They are a cross between field mushrooms and horse mushrooms, of excellent flavour. Sometimes we are lucky enough to have giant puffballs, always in their own place, which is the rough bank of periwinkle and St John's Wort where we once put the hedgehogs. If you catch these puffballs young – though I have had ones as big as a football which were perfect, the flesh

white, clean and firm – they are treasure trove. There's so much of them, because of the close texture, that you can share them round. They make superb soup, chopped, mixed with a little onion, simmered in milk or stock, put through the liquidizer when tender, finished with cream and herbs. Or to stuff a chicken, chopped with a little bacon, onion and beaten egg. Or lightly cooked and added to an omelette – or to any casserole, stew, or game pie.

And this time of year, when the sunlight deepens to make red bars across the timbers in the kitchen wall, I automatically make ratatouille. Blanche Knopf told me that this Provençal vegetable stew was correctly made by cooking all the vegetables separately, and then combining them. She named the famous chef who had told her this, but I foolishly forget. Blanche and her husband Alfred Knopf were Ralph's American publishers until her death and his retirement. Unlike most large and prestigious publishers, they had built up their firm in one generation. Mary McCarthy described Blanche as the one great lady of world publishing, generally a man's world. Tiny, brittle and steely-strong, some people found her formidable. Possibly because I met her first in my own house, when she and Alfred came down to visit us on Ralph's joining them – and because we later stayed many times at their house in Westchester – I not only admired her greatly, but became very fond of both of them. I remember Alfred in the exotic, colourful clothes he favoured, getting out of the car at our front door on that first visit with the enquiring, anticipatory smile of someone who doesn't know what to expect, but hopes it will be fun.

I had cooked for them (between fresh garden things) a Boeuf Stroganoff, I had taken immense pains, bought marvellous beef, done everything right . . . except I didn't realize you cut the meat up into strips; I served the fillets whole. I grew cold with horror when I realized, long after, how I had blundered. But these two well-known gourmets never batted an eyelid. Alfred had two helpings, and remarked that he had never seen Blanche (who seldom ate anything) eat so much. What kindness!

I have since eaten Boeuf Stroganoff prepared by a Russian cook for a Russian family, and that was different from any version I have seen elsewhere. At one time Ralph had an agent in Paris who was a white Russian, and he said to us, 'Everyone's taking you out to eat French food, I wondered if you'd like to come to our house and have a Russian lunch?' The Stroganoff was a drier dish, not sloppy; the thinner-than-usual strips of meat were piled up into a mound in the centre of the platter; the sour cream with mushrooms and onion bound the meat, and it was perfectly moist, but there was no loose sauce surrounding it.

The Knopfs had extremely close connections in France, and published a number of leading French authors – Camus, for example. Blanche was his executor and had just broken her hip at the time of his death; characteristically, she had a long silver pin put through it and flew to France to look after his affairs. They also showed great daring in publishing in America some very forward-looking books – Shreiber's *Lieutenant en Algérie*, for example; Blanche, with her Dior clothes, great rings, and profile of Elizabeth the First, and Alfred, honorary member of various epicurian societies (he had a fine French cook at home in Westchester at that time). They introduced us to Alexandre Dumaine and his wife Jeanne. Dumaine was elected by his peers as the premier chef of France; but Alfred wanted us to meet them as friends, to get to know them, not just go to Saulieu to eat. He said, 'In the opinion of many of us they are the nicest couple in France.'

So next time we were over there we drove to that simple-seeming hotel on the corner of the little town, to which people who cared about food had beaten a path from every corner of the world, and nosed round the back, looking for somewhere to park. Inside a barn, we saw through the open door a slight woman in a grey cardigan bending forward towards a nervous-looking Alsatian and holding out a dish, coaxing it to eat. She looked up and greeted us; by some instinct we guessed, 'Madame Dumaine?'

We stayed long enough to have the dishes you order two days in advance; *Poulet en Vapeur*, for instance, which comes to table in an earthenware pot sealed with a strip of pastry. When this was pulled off and the lid lifted, the smell was ineffable. '*Mais, madame . . . simplement, il sent le poulet. Je n'ai jamais senti . . .*' Jeanne Dumaine, who was standing beside us for the serving, laughed, and said, '*Oui, madame – l'âme d'un poulet!*'

We talked much to Alexandre and Jeanne Dumaine, only

indirectly about food – though she did say once, 'Alexandre sometimes has to complicate dishes more than he thinks right, but the
tourists expect it, or else they think they are not getting their
money's worth.' Actually their prices were not high considering
their prestige. One evening a young American officer drove up,
with his wife and two children in the car. He read the menu, and
possibly glimpsed the lovingly-signed photographs of Margot
Fonteyn, the Rainiers, the Oliviers, discreetly tucked behind
pillars, and was going away. Madame went out to him and said,
'Monsieur, we have a *prix fixe*, of course, and for the children it
would be quite different.' So they stayed, happily wondering what
unexpected glory they had discovered on their journey.

This deliberate simplicity and approachability – in such contrast to his failed competitors for the proud top title! – has gone
now. Since his retirement the Cote d'Or at Saulieu has had a great
facelift to make it like all the others – what people expect. They
still use his recipes, but I am told more elaborately presented –
what people expect! I learned so much there, not about dishes, that
would be too difficult, but about what matters in food. The
apparent – apparent – simplicity of the finished dish, all the choice,
skill, judgment, finesse, hidden in the making. The supreme im-
portance of the quality of the ingredients. All one can learn is a
standard; and by it to recognize and reject the other kind of food,
the elaborately decorated dishes with any unsuitable additions you
can think of, to disguise factory farming and the deep freeze.

When the Dumaines were young, the French government had
sent them to North Africa, to further French interests, so Jeanne
noticed an old Berber locket I was wearing as a fob, and brought
out her own collection of antique Berber jewellery, which put mine
in the shade – she'd had several years to collect, as she said! (From
the tribeswomen of course, in both cases, not from the souks.)

I shall always remember my first glimpse of her, stooping over
the frightened dog. It had been found pressed against the door
when her staff opened the hotel in the morning, deliberately
abandoned from a passing car. '*C'est cruauté, madame, c'est un
crime!*' One of her staff was taking it to her parents, the hotel's
corner position was not safe. Other fugitives had arrived at that
door: the Dumaines had been on the escape route during the war,

and their technique of concealment had never been discovered.

It is no bad thing to remember a great chef when one is cooking – you go more carefully. I was also pondering Blanche's idea of cooking the ingredients of a ratatouille separately. For once I don't agree with her, I think the flavour must be better if they all blend while cooking, and it is easy to keep them firm and distinct if you add them in order of the hardest first. The quality of the olive oil is important, as it permeates the whole dish. Say a coffee cup full to make a nice big ratatouille for two people who like it – I serve it with fluffy dry boiled rice, as a main dish. First finely sliced onion, a young and juicy one. When it is softened, the aubergines, cubed, unpeeled. Then thinly sliced red and green peppers, then diced courgettes, which cook quickly. When all these are tender but not mushy, add diced and peeled tomatoes – not too many, they are so dominant. Some chopped fresh herbs, basil is perfect, but marjoram will do, salt and pepper to taste, and a pinch of allspice or coriander. They say every woman in Provence uses different proportions of these, the classic and essential vegetables, swearing her way is best. I think additions are a mistake, potatoes make it heavy, mushrooms are lost. The skill is to time it so each thing is perfectly cooked, none over-cooked, and the oil absorbed (but if you have some oil left in the pan, lift the vegetables out with a perforated slice, and use the flavoured oil for something else). If something goes wrong and you end up with the sort of featureless slush one gets ladled out in restaurants as an extra to a batch of frozen vegs, then squash it up and pretend you meant it for a sauce, or to add to a soup. It is such a beautiful dish, every vegetable retaining its colour. I cut out a superb colour photograph of ratatouille and pasted it on the cover of a book I bought to stick recipes in, the summer I got married, thinking this was a side of life I ought to start considering.

As the plums turn red on the tree, we see there are far more than we had guessed. The ladder stays against the tree now, to be picked daily. Verena bottles the perfect ones for winter pies. Those damaged by birds-followed-by-wasps, are for eating now. I cut out the damage, peel and stone, and pile them into a golden mound on a dish, sprinkle with sugar and a drop of Kirsch, cover and put in the fridge till wanted. They are good with cream, yoghurt, or a quite sour cream cheese, such as pommel or demi-sel.

We only grow runner beans which never have strings, pick them small and cook them whole, like haricots verts, which they follow. Lightly cooked, so they still snap when bent, I serve them alone as a first course with butter and pepper and salt and herbs. Cucumbers I am reluctant to cook, as their essential quality is to be cool. For a change, not because it is better, I sometimes make cucumber balls with my little French scoop, bought long ago in Paris; plunge them into boiling water till hot through, no more; pile them in bowls with sour cream (also heated), cover with finely grated cheese, and put under the grill till the cheese has melted, and serve instantly. They do still taste of cucumber!

It seems a pity to cook tomatoes while they are still coming in fresh from the garden. Verena bottles them with great success, and also makes a lovely purée for winter sauces and soups. Now, I slice them thinly and sprinkle with olive oil, black pepper, a little sugar, adding salt only at the last minute before eating. Their own juice seems to make lemon or vinegar unnecessary. Tomatoes just picked are as delicious to eat as any fruit. I'm sure they are best eaten alone, or as the main ingredient – perhaps with their own garnishes, black olives, anchovy fillets, chopped hard-boiled egg, nuts; it appals me to find tomato coulis used to smother delicate-flavoured things like trout or courgette, which you then can't taste at all.

In September, Reg sows winter radish and the winter lettuce Kwiek, which will be planted out under cloches, and also takes geranium cuttings.

I try to get our evening meal ready earlier now, to beat the westering sun drawing ever back from the summerhouse, and be in time to join Ralph there for a few minutes before it gets cool and dusk.

When I go out the light is thick and golden and the grass crossed with shadows. The japonica quinces are turning yellow on the wall of the house at the back of the border, and the pyrancantha berries red. The tall white tobacco plants stretch out and are luminous, and their scent drifts about the garden. The swallows are massing on the telegraph wires.

# OCTOBER

# OCTOBER

'Oh the golden sheaf, the rustling
treasure armful!'

GEORGE MEREDITH

We saw the house first in October. After all our searching we recognized her at once. Yes, this was for us. (Who said, speaking for all house-seekers, 'When you find her you will know her, the only she'?) The owner had to re-sell, sadly, because the sale of his old house had fallen through. His daughter, with a girl-friend and an Airedale, were camping in a few rooms to show it to people. We talked in the little room which is now my sitting-room, and one of the girls, leaning back on the low window seat, put her elbow through a pane of the mullion window with its inserts of pre-Reformation glass.

'Oh dear, we'll have that mended of course.' When they'd shown us the house, they invited us to wander round the garden. We stood by the sundial in autumn sunshine, looking at the long uneven black and white house with its irregular roof of red tiles and beautiful chimneys, and I noticed Ralph's hand holding a cigarette was trembling as it rested on the stone. The carving of a long, lithe Scandinavian dog leaped out from one corner of the house – wildly incongruous, but they are the sign of a happy home, and we have never disturbed him. It is part of the life of all old houses that different owners bring back souvenirs from strange places. On a low bit of roof the yellow tufty lichen had naturalized, which is said to be a protection against witches. I remember the garden was all golden, yellow leaves on the trees and on the ground. It had an air of peace and seclusion, the sense of being a world complete in itself, which a garden and its house should have. Tall trees enclosed it.

I didn't take it in in any detail, which was perhaps as well; it had been neglected between owners, and someone had planted wild flowers in the borders. They had filled the four beds round the sundial with celandine and many, many man-hours and woman-hours would be spent before those bunches of little white bulbs were eradicated and we could plan and plant there. Our occasional visitors helped. I remember a cousin of mine, pregnant at the time, rising a little heavily to her feet saying, 'I've been wondering in what way my first-born may resemble a celandine.'

October is a glowing month. There's a saying in Suffolk, 'The heel of the year is always golden.' It is the month when the last of the summer crops overlap with the first of the autumn season in a continuing abundance. I try to put off starting each new crop, hoarding for the leaner months ahead.

It is the storing month – for everyone. Reg once moved a cupboard in the garage and found concealed behind it a pyramid of apples so well-built you couldn't knock it down, but had to take away each apple separately. A rat had built it. What extraordinary skill! And what a labour, to bring each one quite a distance, and place it so carefully. It seemed a shame to demolish it.

Reg is harvesting, harvesting; Yiwara beside him, anticipating the crop being carried and which way the barrow is going, so she can always trot ahead of him. They are lifting and storing the various kinds of potatoes; the later apples; hanging up the cabbages, red and white and green. The onions and shallots have lain on the sunny path in front of the summerhouse to dry, and Reg is stringing them. He uses a different method from the French onion-sellers, and I think better, as you can pull out any one you choose without loosening the others, and the long bunches look so attractive. A whole shelf in the store cupboard is filled with golden gourds, and some white custard marrows, for winter soups. A higher shelf is full of the last tomatoes, covered with newspaper to ripen them (they will last into December). The chicory is growing through its clamp and has to be earthed up.

Reg's Dutch sprouts are ready, growing in a perfect and very decorative spiral. The first celery, the first celeriac, artichokes. There's a wonderful crop of hazelnuts. They keep best packed into biscuit tins, in their husks, and sprinkled with salt, put on the stone floor of the larder. They are still full and white in January.

It was in October, I think, that Reg once knocked on the study door and said, 'Come and look. I've got something marvellous.' As he never disturbs·Ralph at work, he knew it must be worth seeing, so he went, collecting me on the way.

Outside the garden, on the edge of the field, Reg had been forking a pile of dead vegetation onto a bonfire when he noticed a large hedgehog, curled into a ball, hibernating. He moved it, and then at a lower level, buried deeper in the leaves, found two half-grown hedgehogs, presumably the spring litter. Deeper still, he found another adult, we thought the female; and below her, in the position of greatest safety, the best protected of all, three very small ones – the second family of the year.

What to do with them? Out here they were now vulnerable to children, dogs, cats. Their chosen pile could not be put back. We must get them into the safety of the garden. I ran into the house and got several big carrier bags, and gently pushed the sleeping hedgehogs, with as much of the soft rubble as possible, into them. We took them into the garden and decanted them gently into a bank of St John's Wort and periwinkle which covered them completely. For the rest of the day we kept our dog in (it was long before Yiwara's time). When we visited the bank there were a lot of grunts and scuffling and the foliage moved as they burrowed deeper. We put a bowl of milk near. Next day it had gone and all was quiet. Ever since then we have had hedgehogs in the garden. Much better than pesticides for controlling slugs and snails!

The larder shelves are being replenished with Verena's preserves; strawberry and raspberry jams; jars of little green gooseberries for sorbets and fools; larger bottles of Victoria plums. Bottles of tomatoes. Spiced peaches from her own tree, we have none. The kitchen smells delicious the day she does this! We use an old recipe once cut from a newspaper, rather tattered now, pinned into a book. We've tried others, but like this best. The proportions are: with two pounds of peaches, not too ripe, half a pint of white vinegar, one pound of demerara sugar, cloves, a short cinnamon stick, a bay leaf. Dip the peaches into boiling water, then skin them, halve and stone. Stick four cloves into each half peach (more if they're very large). Put vinegar, sugar and cinnamon into pan, heat slowly, stirring till sugar has melted. Put the peaches

in, bring gently to boil, cook on low heat till tender but not soft. Lift out with a perforated spoon and put into hot preserving jars, pour the hot syrup over and seal. They don't want to be used at once. Last year's are better than this year's, two years old or more, even better. They go dark and rich and succulent, and add great glamour to cold meats. The jars should not be too full of peaches as the syrup is so good; each jar has its cinnamon sticks and bay leaf, which I put in the dish when serving.

Our earliest apples are the best cookers but they don't last, so we make the most of them at once. They are yellow-green, silky, conical – a very pretty apple, and sometimes very large. We don't know the names of any of our apples, except the Coxes, as the trees were here when we came. (A friend, curious about a particularly good cooking apple in his garden – and in many local gardens – sent one up to the head apple-growing authority to find out what variety it was; back came the answer, 'This is an old Suffolk cooking apple.' So why bother? How quaint, by the way, that people not interested in the subject, think that because the French don't designate different varieties for cooking, but cook 'dessert' apples, we make do with something inferior! On the contrary, we grow certain varieties for cooking because they cook much better than the kinds we eat raw. The dreary standardization of the Common Market will probably rule out our cooking varieties, as so many of our crops have been ruled out, but at least we have the old trees all over England – and the stocks have been established overseas.)

These fluffy, pale, early apples I core and stuff with mincemeat and bake; it's worth running the point of a knife round the middle of each apple when you core them, so when cooked the top half of the skin lifts off whole like a little cap for you to add the cream. As well as pies, it's even worth making apple-fluff with these; peel and core and simmer with very little water, add a little cider or wine if you have it; I like the raw cane sugar muscovado, soft and dark, best; it has flavour as well as sweetness, and it smells so nice. I add a pinch of allspice. When tender, put through the liquidizer. When cold, pile it up in the centre of a dish and sprinkle with chopped nuts, or grated chocolate, or raw blackberries. (This freezes into a delicate and unusual ice, either mixed with cream or by itself if, when the apples are ripe, it's still warm enough to want ices!) It's important not to let the blackberry season slip by without going to our woods and picking enough blackberries for Verena to make purée, either for sorbets or as a sauce over other fruits – peaches or melon, for instance. Our melons in the garden are good this year. We grow cantaloups, Ogen and Dutch net, under cloches.

We have a tree of large but very hard pears. Peeled and cored and quartered, I pack them into a fireproof dish with a fitting lid, sprinkle with muscovado sugar and a little allspice, pour over them as much red wine as I can spare (from my half-bottles in the fridge) then top up with water to half-cover; put at the back of the lower Aga oven and forget – leave overnight at least. They go mahogany coloured, tender, almost candied. I don't think it's any good trying this without a stove that gives you permanent low heat.

The peppers continue, big and red. There are still aubergines. I go on with these final summer things and turn a blind eye to new season's crops just beginning – time enough for them. In October Reg sows early peas, sweet peas, and the winter lettuce Kloek (to grow under cloche). Is it not this eternal looking-forward in a garden, which lifts the heart?

The dahlias dominate the garden now, with late michaelmas daisies and iceplant in the border, and a few clumps of red chrysanthemums. I've always been half-hearted about chrysanthemums, which I don't really like; I must overcome this, they are so useful – they never seem to die. Is this why they're rather depressing?

The golden quinces on the japonicas along the wall at the back of the border are gorgeous, massed bunches of them this year, very large. Picked for the house, they greet you in the morning, after being shut up all night in a warm room, with a fresh, delicious scent. I mix them with dangling sprays of the big 'imitation cherries' from the malus tree, which is a blazing sight in the garden now, and scarlet leaves from the guelder rose – these soon shrivel, but are irresistibly attractive. A few late roses complete these bowls. The prunus autumnalis are already spangled with white spring-like blossom, though the long red and yellow leaves still hang on the trees, making one of the prettiest sights of the year. There are still a lot of roses.

Now the chairs are brought in from the summerhouse, and ash

logs from the woods are stacked beside the back door –

> For ash brown or ash green
> Make a fire fit for a queen.

I move the winter primroses back to their corners near the house, some of them are already showing colour, which is helpful as you can mix them better. The geraniums and fuschias and begonias are taken to the greenhouse for the winter, and wallflowers replace them in the tubs beside the house and the summerhouse. But still the year has a lingering mellowness.

Then the clocks are put back from Summer Time, and suddenly it's dark early. We start lighting the drawing-room fire for tea and drawing the curtains.

# NOVEMBER

# NOVEMBER

'Is it the mist, or the dead leaves,
Or the dead men – November eves?'

FLECKER

Verena thinks November is the worst month of the year;
'December there's Christmas to look forward to.
January the evenings begin to draw out and you can
look forward to the spring. But November . . .'

I don't mind this muted, waiting month so much. It can be just
dark grey, but it has its beauties too; the lacework of black twigs
against the apricot sunsets we have so often at this time of year –
exactly the colour of the few remaining leaves. The autumnalis is
massed with buds all over, and this year they are opening on the
tree. But for fear of a sudden frost (such as always takes dahlias in a
night) I cut branches for the house. They open first in a jug on top
of a cupboard in the kitchen, but soon we have this false-spring all
over the house. I've a copper bowl in the hall full of it, mixed with
the old-rose spindle berries from the woods and a few sprays of
yellow jasmine. This is already out in brilliant yellow showers on
the summerhouse, on the west wall of the house and draped up the
laburnum tree by the gate. The japonica quinces are hanging on
well, turning a darker gold, and the fruits on the malus tree (oddly
enough they turn lighter, from crimson to scarlet), are a brilliant
sight blazing in the sunshine. Now the dahlias have gone I regret
not having been more serious about chrysanthemums. Perhaps I
could get some in fresher colours, so they don't always seem to me
in the same category as a cold in the head – only their smell of damp
mossy woods is attractive. There's a colourful scatter of late
roses (Autumn Delight is still fully clothed), and the white tobacco
plants still shine out, too ragged now to pick, but lighting the
garden. Primroses are out in little pockets of the rockery. The

robins sing incessantly, glad to have the garden clear of all those migrants, perhaps.

In November I arrange for the winter the circular vase round the Chinese lamp in the corner of the drawing-room. This stays till early spring; it's the only 'dead' arrangement I do, as I prefer pot plants. I try to make it very airy-fairy and light. Just long trails of Old Man's Beard (picked before it gets too fluffy and put in glycerine and water for some time so it doesn't drop), and a mass of scarlet berries of the English iris. This has naturalized itself in wild corners of the garden; you don't notice its tiny brown flowers, but in autumn its brilliant seed pods not only rise above the blade-shaped leaves, but lie heavy below them, and in the vase they bend gracefully on their thin stalks. They last till spring, shiny and not dropping if they, too, are put in glycerine and water first. Then one or two sprays of beech leaves, dark brown, to give weight and contrast (I try to remember to put these in glycerine in August, as they take better). I add a few long streamers of a small-leaved, bright green ivy to freshen the arrangement – these I renew from time to time. After that, anything I can think of – tall delicate grasses, a few flat golden achillea heads, one or two Jack-o'-Lanterns (Cape gooseberries) which we have a bank of in the woods: one superb mullein head, some sprays of dead astilbe – very pretty. As this winter arrangement is with us for so long, I try to make it exuberant and shapely, the Old Man's Beard curving up and down against the wooden beams in the wall behind it, and the iris seeds really in showers.

This is the squirrel month, one thinks of saving things. And now the trees are bare, one sometimes sees a wild leap, and squirrels running along a branch. Yiwara (and Ralph) hate squirrels, she can never forgive them for climbing above her, but I am glad to see anything alive and free in our poison-soaked countryside.

We very seldom have a good walnut crop. This is traditionally a walnut village and Reg remembers when he was a child everyone had them. But he discovered something interesting about walnuts a few years ago: that the buds are only fertile for a very short time and if the weather conditions are not right at that moment, the season's crop is lost. But why didn't this happen as frequently in the past? A change in the weather pattern?

We discussed this with Tony Stokes, who confirmed the change. He used to come to breakfast on Sundays – sometimes. He owned Hintlesham, before Robert Carrier bought it and turned it into a most glamorous restaurant. Tony had invented and ran the Hintlesham Festival. He was a Georgian host at heart, but couldn't afford to indulge this privately. The Festival was a way of filling this large, fascinating Elizabethan house and its grounds with people. The theatre was in the garden at the back, the swimming pool became the orchestra pit. After the performance, Tony made a little speech inviting the audience to have 'an arboreal experience'. This was a walk through the grounds which he had floodlit – quite beautifully; he was a brilliant engineer; it was the only floodlighting that never shone in your face!

Unexpectedly he said to me one day, 'Do you have breakfast on Sundays?' I explained it was the one day in the week when, yes, we did have breakfast, a real cooked, leisurely breakfast. 'May I come and have it with you?' Tony asked. 'I go to Mass and then have a perfectly horrid breakfast in a pub. I'm sure yours would be much better.'

So – when he remembered, when he woke up in time, when we were at home – this rubicund-faced white head on a tall body with a rolling gait would make its way up our drive on Sunday mornings. Ralph had stipulated that he would be welcome provided he didn't discuss the Festival at breakfast. He always honoured this, and barred from his beloved obsession, was a most entertaining talker, with an infinite range of subjects.

On his death Hintlesham House was threatened with destruction, that lovely house with all its history. To the delight of everyone who knew it, Robert Carrier bought it – restored it, cherished it, made it his home. (Alas, he has now sold it.) But we miss our engaging eccentric at Sunday breakfast!

There are excellent lettuces under cloches, tiny 'spring' onions and small salad carrots as well as big ones, and radishes. Now at lunch time it is soup again; celeriac, leek, the gourds on the shelf . . . But didn't I talk about them before – all the winter vegetables that are coming round again? So the cycle of the year is closing.

An invaluable new (to us) crop is the chicory described in the catalogues as Sugar Loaf – not to be confused with Chicory

Witloof, the Belgian endive. These enormous things are like a giant cos lettuce which has had a slight affair with a very tender cabbage. Peel off the outer leaves and you have succulent, tender, fleshy leaves, pale green to white. Slice very thinly, or just tear apart, dress with vinaigrette, adding chopped apple, grated carrot, finely-sliced leek if you wish. Or treat as coleslaw, dressed with sour cream or yoghurt and mayonnaise.

The last and best of the fungus come now – Boletus Edulus (cepes). We sometimes find them in our woods. Firm, thick, with brown spongy gills, they deserve to be a dish on their own. The classic way to cook any fungus to preserve its full flavour is to wipe, not wash, it, remove stalks for soup, lay upside down on a flat, well-buttered dish; put a blob of butter – or sprinkle with oil – add salt, pepper and a squeeze of lemon, cover tightly and bake till just tender. Serve from this dish, adding only chopped parsley, to eat with crusty bread. But another pleasant way is to slice thickly, and cook in butter and oil with a little chopped garlic and a lot of parsley. They can then be served on toast, adding very thin rashers of crisply grilled bacon if you wish to make a bigger dish. Of course mushrooms can be used in the same way, if they are the big open dark-gilled ones (wild mushrooms picked in the fields) not the little white tasteless button mushrooms.

We once chanced upon a group of French people eagerly picking some fungus and laying them lovingly on a sheet spread in the boots of their cars. This was in the high Causse area, in the middle of southern France, where the long limestone ridges run out to the sea; the bare grassland where the sheep graze from whose milk, during the lambing season, Roquefort is made (and a host of other blue cheeses as good but not famous). The limestone caverns play a very important part in the maturing of these cheeses, the humidity being maintained by an underground lake. Kid gloves come from this area too, from the skins of the lambs.

They were picking in light woodland, and seeing our interest they charmingly told us, 'les bolets roses!' and indicated where there were plenty more. Apparently these pink boletus are very rare, of exquisite flavour and much sought after. We took ours home to the little auberge we were staying in, and they were received with rapture. We thought they'd cook them for us for our supper . . .

but oh, no! They saw us off next day with home-made paté, bottled preserves – they'd have given us anything, but never a single *bolet rose* did they part with!

Another year we were staying with friends in Normandy, near Lisieux, at the time of the annual *jours micrologiques* – mushroom time. We picnicked in the woods with a friend of theirs who was an acknowledged expert on the subject, and I have a photograph of us all sitting round him under a big tree, surrounded by the spoils we had gathered. Many varieties were familiar to us from English woods, but some were quite strange, including one which resembled cauliflower. Then we drove to Lisieux to see the *fête micrologique*. In the large town hall the main room was filled with tables, covered with white cloths, on which edible fungi were laid out, all labelled, beautifully arranged. Each represented the product of a different area. I doubt if there are many more varieities in France or Switzerland than in England; they just take the subject more seriously.

So few people ever taste a potato – it's always subordinated to other flavours. A humble but very cosy supper dish, or accompaniment to another dish, is stuffed baked potatoes. This depends for its excellence on the quality of the potato; large floury ones are needed. I scrub and bring to the boil from cold, simmer very briefly, strain, and when dry paint with oil. This makes the skin deliciously crisp. Bake till soft (test with fork or squeeze). Cut in half longways, scoop out floury part, leaving a neat shell, and beat with butter or cream, pepper and salt, till light and foamy. Then beat in whatever occurs to you. I like chopped raw celery. Put back in the shells, sprinkle with coarsely chopped walnuts or hazelnuts, dot with butter and put into hot oven till crusty on top. The celery will be hot but not cooked, keeping its crisp texture. Sometimes I mix into the whipped-up and seasoned potato enough of Verena's tomato purée to turn it pink (having used butter, not cream, to avoid mushiness). Pile strips of red pepper, or grated carrot and paprika, on top and bake again till hot, then surround with lightly grilled tomato quarters. Baby clams, now back on the market, with chives or a little shallot, are another good filling, and a taste of curry paste beaten in with them.

A French girl who used to spend school holidays with my mother and me used to make us a dish she said she made at home.

In a shallow fireproof dish, well-buttered, she would arrange a layer of thinly sliced potato, then a layer of thinly sliced onion, then a thick sprinkle of grated cheese (or very thin slices of cheese). Repeat these layers till dish is full, finishing with potatoes, then top with cheese, dot with butter, and pour milk, the creamier the better, to a little below the top. Bake in oven till cooked through and crusty on top, and all the milk absorbed.

Hot potato salad is a dish people wolf up and leave the dish as clean as a dog's. Slightly undercook waxy potatoes; while still hot (wear rubber gloves), dice if too big to slice – I can always slice our Aura. Dress with olive oil, enough to coat but not saturate, rock salt and freshly ground black pepper. Add finely chopped mild onion, parsley, chives. Then let your imagination run riot. Add, for instance, sliced mushrooms lightly poached; chopped anchovy fillets; strips of the last green peppers if you still have any in the fridge, crumbled crisply grilled lean bacon, grated carrot, chopped olives, black and green. Squeeze lemon juice or white wine vinegar over it, alternatively fold in mayonnaise thinned with sour cream. Cover tightly with tinfoil and leave in lower oven till hot through. It will wait for you, but not too long.

Now that frozen vegetables have made it the custom to offer several, of little taste, I think interest is swinging back to serving one vegetable cooked with care. The soft green cabbage, for instance, its larger leaves lightly torn apart, the others whole, washed but not dried, tossed in a pan of melted butter, then a lid put on, and left on a very low heat for a few minutes to cook in the buttery steam, shaken frequently and taken off when tender but not limp, sprinkled with salt, pepper and nutmeg or allspice – this is a lovely accompaniment to almost anything. You can trim it with a little chopped apple, or a few tiny onions, but I think the point really is to find out what it tastes like by itself.

A friend gave me a recipe the other day, because I'd enjoyed the dish so much at her house. She had chopped, into quite large pieces, mushrooms, apples and tomatoes; cooked them lightly in butter, then poured hot dry cider over them. She served this with grilled sausages and foamy mashed potato, but I can imagine it giving freshness and tang to many meals. She'd invented it on the spur of the moment, just before the party.

I heard of a curious Provencal recipe (rather out of its country – we were north of Le Puy!) passing through La Chaise-Dieu in winter – to me a bleak, steep town of winding stone alleys below its huge Gothic cathedral. I'm interested that other people retain the same memory of La Chaise-Dieu that we do; the discreetly handled, but so-frequent urinating of its men, making the snow everywhere discoloured. We sat on a little, glassed-in iron balcony in wicker chairs, eating the smallest trout I have ever seen; tiny trout from the mountain streams, but Ralph swears they were the sweetest trout he has ever tasted. They also have some very local vin rosé; nameless, it never leaves home, but it was far better than that rather indeterminate wine usually is.

The recipe was described to me as a *bouillabaise sans poisson*, a frugal housewife's warm and filling dish. It is called *borgue*. You cook chopped onion and garlic in oil, add chopped tomato, orange peel and fennel, saffron, pepper and salt. When they have cooked a little, add potatoes thinly sliced, and cover deeply with water. Cook till potatoes are tender but still firm, then poach eggs, as many as there are people, in the liquid. Strain the liquid over pieces of toast, arrange the potatoes on another plate, then the eggs on top, sprinkle with parsley. Real bouillabaise I have noticed, on its coast of origin, is often served with the liquid (soup) and the solids served separately. I have never tried this dish because I hate poached eggs, I pass it on as an oddity.

Now we have evenings so calm and lovely we can't leave them, but go on working in the garden till the colours are lost in a faint amethyst mist and light lingers only in a pink glow on top of the church tower and in the embers of the sweet-smelling bonfire. Tidying up the border I dislodge a clump of little brown crocus bulbs and hold next spring in my hand. There are mornings of white frost, but it must come late and be light because the autumn-alis is undamaged, still a white shower under the dark gold leaves of a weeping willow – they hang on longer than on the tall ones. I've never known the blossoms go on so late. Reg is trying an interesting comparison – noting down the temperature every day from the thermometer outside the front door, and comparing it with the temperature on the same date last year. Yiwara must go on giving him notebooks for Christmas, the results are so rewarding.

By the end of the month the frosts sharpen and the sunsets go fiery. On the afternoon of 30 November we drove over to Cant's Nurseries at Colchester to collect some roses we'd ordered to replace last winter's losses. It gets dark before four o'clock now, so we went on putting in the roses as long as we could see, helped by the light from a huge full moon which rose slowly over the gate at the end of the garden; while exactly at the opposite end the sunset sky suffused the whole west with a breathtaking red glow. The garden was framed between the blaze at one end and the great pale moon at the other.

My head was down to the last rose when Ralph said, 'This has come up quickly!' I looked up, and in those few minutes a wall of fog had enclosed us, as thick and still as a Dickensian London fog, shutting out everything. I could only just see to collect my tools. Firelight flickered through the drawing-room window, Ralph had gone in ahead of me to light it for tea. I went in the back way in my muddy gumboots and nearly fell over Yiwara, shut in the boiler room to dry her paws.

# DECEMBER

# DECEMBER

'Christmas Eve, and twelve of the clock.
"Now they are all on their knees,"
An elder said as we sat in a flock
By the embers in hearthside ease.

'We pictured the meek mild creatures where
They dwelt in their strawy pen,
Nor did it occur to one of us there
To doubt they were kneeling then.

'So fair a fancy few would weave
In these years! Yet, I feel,
If someone said on Christmas Eve,
"Come; see the oxen kneel

"In the lonely barton by yonder coomb
Our childhood used to know,"
I should go with him in the gloom,
Hoping it might be so.'

THOMAS HARDY (The Oxen)

December is an exciting month, I think, even apart from Christmas and my birthday (Sagittarius, of course). You suddenly find yourself looking forward to things you'll be doing next year, as if a curtain had been drawn from a window. December this year was incredibly mild; open, calm days of sunshine and pale blue skies. Never before had the autumnalis bloomed up to Christmas – and the profusion of vegetables still in the open!

I used to be terrified of Christmas. Not as a child; my mother with her own special magic made it an enchanted time even in the most bare and lonely circumstances. But growing up as an only child, no relatives, no home of our own, I had no precedent to draw upon now. What should one do? Every newspaper and magazine carried pages full of lists of elaborate preparations. What was this enormous ritual everyone was supposed to be working towards?

One year soon after we came here, sitting by the fire over tea in mid-December, Ralph said, 'What are we doing for Christmas? Anything?' I felt so mortified, so inadequate, I got up and went to the phone and rang up everyone we knew in the neighbourhood – not many in those days – and asked them to come and have a drink with us on Christmas Eve. Rather to my surprise they all accepted. It was a small enough party to hold in the drawing-room, I don't think we'd opened the hall out yet, and when they were leaving one rather charming old boy said, 'We've stayed much longer than we meant to. That shows it was a good party!'

So that's how it started. Whenever we're at home (roughly every other year) we have a party on Christmas Eve, to me the most magical day of Christmas. It grew as the number of our friends grew, and when we opened up the hall we held it there and spread through the house.

We decorate with evergreens; manufactured trimmings would look silly in this old house, but evergreens are at home – bringing in the forest as in medieval times, and earlier, to honour the Green Man. Ralph's mother, long ago, arriving with his father to spend Christmas with us, asked kindly if she could do anything to help. 'Decorate the hall,' Ralph said instantly. She drew a deep breath, then said, 'Bring me a lot of that very long-stranded small-leaved ivy hanging over the wall outside the garage. A lot; really a lot.' She twined strands round each banister, both sides of the staircase, fitting into the turnings of the finely-carved wood, dainty enough to look through to the lights beyond. We put holly round both posts at the bottom, and at the bend of the staircase. I tied the greenery at strategic points with bows of scarlet satin ribbons, leaving long ends. It looked so lovely we've done the same ever since. Ralph used to dig up a Christmas tree from our woods and put it in a tub in front of the spit in the further fireplace, and I decorated it with a mass of tiny paper parasols which I'd bought in San Francisco (at a shop which described itself as 'The Largest Emporium in the World'!). They looked like a flight of butterflies. But now our trees have got too big, so this year Ralph arranged sweeping branches of lacy spruce stuck into logs with holes in them, and arching across the embrasure. There's a spotlight on this, and on the luminous John Newton painting over the fire at the other end. Apart from these, we light only with candles.

Ralph invented a very special mull (Mull-Innes). A good wine to start with, and the right additions of liqueur and brandy . . . The year he perfected it we had a friend staying in the house who was extremely interested in wine and had a fine cellar. I went into the kitchen when they were tasting it, drawn by the gorgeous smell. Our friend, putting down his glass, was saying: 'It's very smooth now, Ralph, almost perfection. Do you think . . . if you just *showed* it the brandy once more . . . ?'

I decided to serve a fork supper. I remember ghastly failures – taking some desperate recipe from a newspaper, or just not allowing enough for more people than I was used to. I wonder my friends kept on coming, they were marvellously kind. Why do I always get things wrong so many times before I get them right? One year I thought how pretty candles would look (and how safe!) stuck in wet moss. I hadn't realized the heat would dry out the moss. A moment came when every group of candles in the hall was surrounded by blazing moss – in an old half-timbered house in an old half-timbered village, where care about fire is a built-in, inherited instinct! 'Oh, how pretty!' someone said. Thank God a sailing friend – it would be a sailing friend – quickly and efficiently extinguished them all, smilingly overriding another guest whose only idea was to fling my beautiful arrangements out into the garden.

Another year, having seen how effectively irregular the New York skyline was, I arranged lovely bowls of candles of very varying heights and thicknesses. They did look impressive . . . but the heat of the shorter candles melted the tall ones, nipping them in the middle so they bent down and bowed and curved among the little ones. Again I was in tears and swore 'I'll never, never do this again.'

But I did, and finally got it streamlined. Now I have white candles (big ones, to last) in copper bowls and pans about the hall, stuck into oasis, which I conceal with shells, of which I have a big collection from the Great Barrier Reef and various African beaches; the mother-of-pearl shines in the candlelight. Green candles in the drawing-room, and the picture-lights on; red candles in the dining-room. A log fire in each room.

Ralph's mull is kept hot in a large silver punch bowl on a hot-plate in the hall; Nora's husband Jim, whose birthday it is, comes along and ladles it out, and Nora and Verena go round filling up from jugs. Ralph replenishes from a preserving pan on the Aga in the kitchen. He has placed a floodlight down in the rockery to illuminate the house with its holly ring on the door, and further to welcome people as they walk up the drive he leaves the curtains of his study windows open and the spotlights inside trained onto a wall of books.

During the years when our church bells could not be played because of urgent repairs to the tower a group of village people learned to play carols on the hand-bells, and they came to us on Christmas Eve. At first they weren't very good (sometimes they'd only got together and practised a bit because we'd pleaded how much our friends would like to hear them!), then a charming retired musician offered help and held rehearsals. They became very good indeed. But apart from the lovely sound, the sheer look was so exciting. Suddenly in the middle of the party, they would march in like visitors from another world, timeless, bringing the country with them, bringing the outdoors; in russet clothes, carrying on a tall stand a Tilley lamp (such as had been used to light barns before they were electrified). They would set this up in the space cleared for them at the foot of the stairs, to see the music by, and the circle of harsh white light carved the Suffolk faces into woodcuts; an island in the mellow candle-light of the rest of the room.

Supper is laid out in the dining-room. The main course is always the famous Kersey ham. An old Suffolk cure started in August, and done by the Stiff family for several generations, it is sent far and wide (has been on TV!), and must be ordered long in advance. This is set on a thick oak platter, and Ralph carves enough for thirty or so people before they come. Before this smoked salmon, or smoked haddock mousse, or just more substantial salads than usual. This year I had three: potato and mushroom salad (our Aura potatoes, small, sliced and combined with about a third of their quantity of small mushrooms cooked *à la Grecque*, dressed at the last minute with mayonnaise and yoghurt mixed half and half, and a few chopped spring onions). Then chicory and grapefruit and prawns dressed with sour cream, garnished with mustard-and-cress. And a fresh green salad – the sugar-loaf chicory finely sliced, mixed with some red cabbage previously plunged into boiling water after shredding, then marinaded in French dressing; added to finely-grated raw carrot, chopped apple, finely sliced leeks; add extra French dressing at the last minute.

People pass through the dining-room, fortunately there are two doors, are served by Verena and Nora, help themselves to salads and rolls, then back in the hall take glasses of wine (not the mull) and sit where they like through the house. Hot mince pies are passed round next and I put a Stilton on the chest at the foot of the stairs, with baskets of biscuits and bread. Finally I take round dates stuffed with marzipan – red and green. I can't think why I started making these – because I like them so myself, I suppose, and it's easy to make some extra marzipan when I'm icing the cake.

Now I look forward to our Christmases at home, and enjoy our parties. On Christmas night I have a dinner party of eight or ten. I like Verena to spend Christmas with her family, but she leaves everything superbly ready. As there's all the rest of the year to be original I serve a classic English Christmas dinner, which is a delicious meal if you do it right. I can get a natural, healthy, free-range turkey (so different from those intensively mass-produced things one finds on Cold Tables throughout the year). I use a Normandy stuffing: half of crumbled chestnuts, the other half a mixture of diced apple, celery, leek and a few breadcrumbs, the whole bound with beaten egg; a little sausagemeat at the other end. I infuse the milk for bread sauce in advance, leaving it for some hours with onion and cloves, bay leaf and nutmeg, salt and pepper, so only the breadcrumbs have to be added near the time. Gravy I prepare in advance too from the giblets. We use Majestic potatoes for roasting, and Reg's special sprouts, lightly cooked so they are fresh and firm. The rum butter and brandy sauce I have also made in advance, to accompany Verena's delectable pudding, rich and dark, but light. She is always toasted in her absence over the Christmas pudding. Oddly enough we use for the pudding an old wartime recipe of my mother's – we know it's wartime because it includes the historic phrase, 'Raisins are not included, as there is no issue of them this year'. (We include them, but apart from that I see no reason to try another recipe.) Then the Stilton with our own celery; then dessert – fruit in the olive-wood corbeille we brought from Vence, nuts in the little baskets I brought from Annecy in my schooldays, sweets in the silver dishes my mother had on her dinner table in India – and on the pink-dyed damask tablecloth a centre piece of silver jewry work on pale pink satin, which she brought home with her and somehow hung on to through all the years of packing and unpacking trunks. So all my life is there. With a light fresh first course – this year melon balls and chicory and prawns in sour cream – Ralph offers vodka (we have had champagne in the hall by the fire before dinner). With the main course and the Stilton he serves Beychevelle – but alas, alas! we have now finished the Beychevelle.

Then we go to the drawing-room for coffee in mother's strange old Turkish cups, with the Chinese teaspoons which are the only thing I have that my father gave me, sending them home to me as a baby, from Shanghai, shortly before his death. (But he actually sent handkerchiefs, and they arrived as silver teaspoons, all different . . . strange, the Chinese.)

So now I am not afraid of Christmas any more. I know what to do. Decorate the house and fill it with our friends, to celebrate having a home; try to give it a glow in which people can be happy, imagine a moment's lull in the awful traffics of the world, light a candle against the dark.

The donkey in the field at the end of our garden is a part of my Christmas, and the great square-towered church above us on the hill. Like most old houses, this one has 'runs' inside the masonry which go on from generation to generation, and no one quite gets at them. We have one that starts above my bathroom. Lying in my bath I hear something land with a thud overhead from outside the window, pass over the east bedroom, which is on a lower level – and downstairs in the kitchen I have picked up the continuation of this run, passing overhead until it reaches some space above the store cupboard, which is beyond the boiler room. A rat, I suppose – the one who piled the apples in the garage? I never hear this more than once or twice a season, and always in mid-winter. She never invades the house, or molests me in any way, and I have no wish to molest her. I picture her resting at last beside her colourful store, amassed with such endless labour, looking bright-eyed, satisfied at the red apples and golden quinces, potatoes and hazelnuts; and she too is part of my Christmas.

A few days after Christmas I was getting our dinner when I remembered I'd left my small trug in the garden – I'd been getting moss for the hyacinth bowls. I ran out to get it. It was a calm, mild night. Between Christmas and the New Year there is this curious sense of a pause, as if the earth had hesitated on its axis before tipping forward again. The real hard cold which seals the garden had not struck yet, and in this moment of suspension before its annual withdrawal the garden felt very conscious, very present. I found the trug down by the stream opposite the house and turned to go back. Then I stopped. The house looked absurdly long with lights in all its windows; the drawing-room, my sitting-room, the hall, the dining-room, the kitchen, the boiler room; a gap, then the study lights where Ralph was working. The roof-line was clear against the sky, and away to the right above the cherry trees a slim new moon glittered very white compared to the mellow, yellow house lights. Sometimes a familiar house has a strong presence, if you suddenly see it whole when you weren't thinking about it; as if it were looking back at you.

I've always known there must be a day waiting for me when I should go round the garden for the last time, this exuberant, over-generous garden, never quite under control (or should I not know when it was the last time?) and I've wondered idly what season that would be. Golden autumn, as when we saw it first, glowing with yellow leaves and vivid purple and crimson of the late flowers, and a drift of bonfire smoke; or calm green summer, the air full of willow seeds and sky full of swifts; or spring in a riot of green, daffodils everywhere and the cherries white clouds, all the birds darting about with their beaks full of building materials; or sealed in winter as now, everything hidden, resting, waiting. Which crops would be left when my Aga was cold?

Whoever comes here after us will inevitably simplify for ease of

maintenance, wiping out the pattern. Some day a housing estate may be built over it, as happened to my aunt's garden in Kent. At least I have recorded it.

Chestnut candles are lit again
For the dead who died in spring;
Dead lovers walk the orchard ways,
And the dead cuckoos sing.

Is it they who live and we who are dead?
Hardly the springtime knows
For whom today the cuckoo calls,
And the white blossom blows.

Listen and hear the happy wind
Whisper and lightly pass;
Your love is sweet as hawthorn is,
Your hope green as the grass.

The hawthorn's faint and quickly gone,
The grass in autumn dies;
Put by your life, and see the spring
With everlasting eyes.

WILLIAM KERR

# INDEX OF RECIPES

Eating Round the Year from My Suffolk Garden